Scuba Diving

Jack Jackson

This edition published by Connaught
an imprint of New Holland Publishers (UK) Ltd
First published in 2000 by New Holland Publishers (UK) Ltd
London • Cape Town • Sydney • Auckland

Garfield House, 86-88 Edgware Road
London W2 2EA

80 McKenzie Street
Cape Town 8001
South Africa

Level 1, Unit 4, 14 Aquatic Drive
Frenchs Forest, NSW 2086
Australia

218 Lake Road
Northcote, Auckland
New Zealand

ISBN 978 1 84517 189 6

Publisher: Mariëlle Renssen
Editor: Gill Gordon
Designer: Mark Jubber
Illustrator: Danie Jansen van Vuuren

British consultant: Nick Hanna
Australian consultant: Richard Taylor
New Zealand consultant: Angie Belcher

Reproduction by Hirt & Carter (Cape) Pty Ltd
Printed and bound in Singapore by Craft Print (Pte) Ltd

Disclaimer

This book contains a wealth of information backed by the author's experience over three decades of diving. However, no book is a substitute for experience. No reputable dive shop or operation will refill your scuba cylinder or allow you to hire diving equipment unless you are qualified, or accompanied by an instructor. It is recommended that this book is used in conjunction with training by a recognized recreational diving training agency.

The author and publishers have made every effort to ensure that the information contained in this book was accurate at the time of going to press, they accept no responsibility for any injury or inconvenience sustained by any person using this book or the advice given in it.

Contents

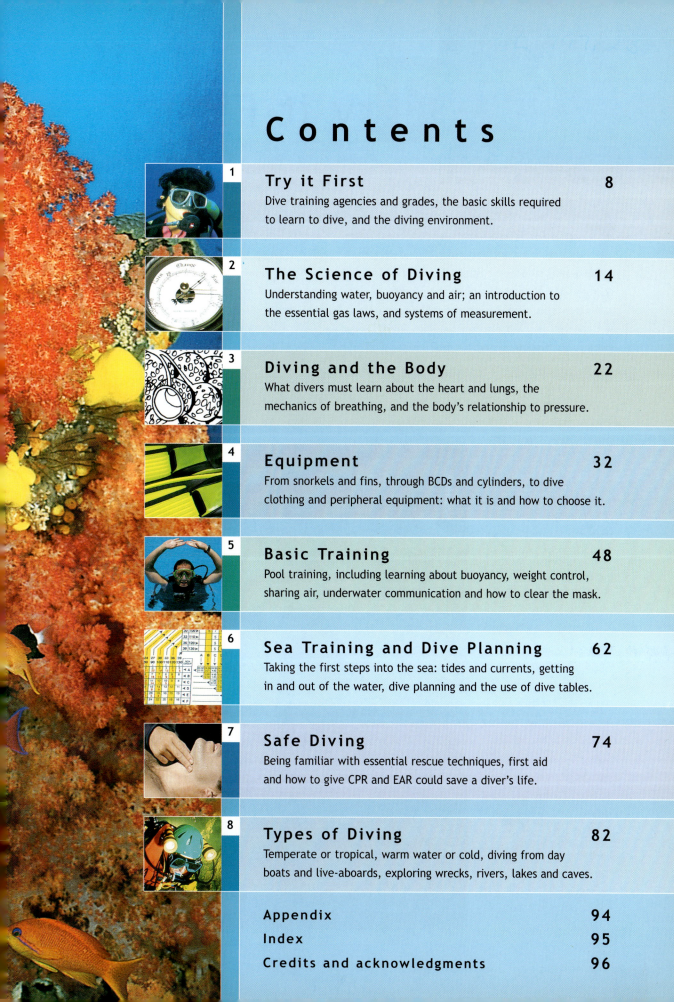

Try it First

the profusion and variety of fish and invertebrates found in both tropical and temperate waters surprises most people the first time they venture underwater with a mask and snorkel.

More amazing is that, unlike on the plains of Africa, you can get very close to the wildlife. Diving is like visiting an aquarium and getting inside with the animals. Few marine animals will swim away, some will even be curious enough to come and inspect you. From tiny plankton to the largest animals in the world, divers can often get within touching distance of them.

In the first 10m (30ft) underwater, there is a remarkable amount of colour. Below that some colours of the light spectrum are filtered out but they can be restored by using an underwater light or photographer's strobe (flash gun).

When you are close to a reef, the underwater world is far from silent. If you stop and listen, the sounds of animals eating or attempting to frighten off others can be quite loud. If you are lucky enough to get close to whales or dolphins, their shrieks, whistles and groans can be felt as well as heard.

Thanks to modern diving equipment, the underwater world is accessible to almost everyone.

People of all ages can enjoy the sport. Children over 12 can begin scuba training, while those as young as eight are allowed to 'try it out' with an instructor in the safety of protected surroundings.

However, diving is equipment-intensive and takes place in an environment that is alien to the human body, so correct and detailed training is essential.

Initially the amount of information that you need to acquire may seem daunting, but by gradually building up your knowledge during organized training, it soon becomes simple and once you understand the theory of diving, then the practice becomes common sense. What matters is that you do enough training to instinctively make the correct reaction if anything goes wrong.

Most people are naturally anxious when they start diving, so you should always begin in a swimming pool or in protected shallow water. Once you are past the initial stage, it is worth completing your dive training in tropical waters. Most training agencies offer courses where you do your initial lessons and training in the classroom and swimming pool, before completing your open-water training in an exotic location where the warm clear water, beautiful corals and brightly-hued fish

ONE OF THE PLEASURES OF SCUBA DIVING IS BEING ABLE TO OBSERVE FISH AT CLOSE QUARTERS, SUCH AS THE SPINECHEEK ANEMONEFISH, OR CLOWNFISH (TOP AND ABOVE) AND POOR KNIGHTS (RIGHT).

command your attention, overcoming any apprehension you might have and increasing your confidence.

Although you must be able to swim, you do not have to be a strong swimmer to dive. If you feel relaxed in the water, can swim 200m (218yd) and tread water for 10 minutes, that is enough so long as you are in average health. A minority of people feel claustrophobic or anxious, breathe heavily or never manage to clear their ears or sinuses, so to make sure that diving is right for you, try it out first before setting off for that long-awaited exotic destination.

All recognized dive training agencies run introductory pool sessions, where an instructor familiarizes would-be divers with the equipment and some of the techniques, and then lets them try diving in shallow water under supervision.

These introductory sessions are normally enough to give a feeling for the sport. If you want to go further, begin by buying the minimum of equipment, just a mask, snorkel, fins and weight belt, and hire the rest from your training operation until you are sure that you wish to continue with the sport.

CLOSE ENCOUNTERS, SUCH AS WITH THIS GIANT GROUPER, AT THE *PRESIDENT COOLIDGE* WRECK IN VANUATU, ARE A DIVING HIGHLIGHT.

Divers slowly develop their experience and skills, so that they can handle themselves in different or more challenging conditions. A diver's prowess is influenced by the experience gained on each of his or her dives. You will learn from both good dives and ones where mistakes have been made. As with all adventure sports there is an element of risk in scuba diving, but this is reduced to acceptable limits by good training.

Equivalent diving grades

There are a number of international dive training agencies all offering similar training under different names. The British Sub-Aqua Club (BS-AC) accepts the following qualifications to be roughly equivalent.

Entry Level:

BS-AC	Club Diver/Ocean Diver
NAUI	Scuba Diver & Advanced Diver
PADI	Open Water Diver & Advanced Open Water Diver
SAA	Open Water Diver
SSI	Open Water & Advanced Open Water Diver
SDI	Open Water Scuba Diver

These qualifications do not usually include rescue training.

Second Level:

BS-AC	Sports Diver
NAUI	Scuba Rescue Diver
PADI	Rescue Diver
SAA	Club Diver
SSI	Advanced Open Water Diver with Stress & Rescue Speciality
SDI	Rescue Diver

These qualifications must include rescue training.

Third Level:

BS-AC	Dive Leader
NAUI	Master Scuba Diver
PADI	Divemaster
SAA	Dive Leader
SSI	Master Diver
SDI	Divemaster

Higher Grades:

Any higher level of qualification than listed above such as:

BS-AC	Advanced Diver
SAA	Dive Supervisor

Legend:

BS-AC	British Sub-Aqua Club
NAUI	National Association of Underwater Instructors
PADI	Professional Association of Diving Instructors
SAA	Sub-Aqua Association
SSI	Scuba Schools International
SDI	Scuba Diving International

VIEWED FROM SPACE, THE OCEANS dominate earth. Covering the largest portion of our planet, they provide us with food, a large area for recreation, and have an important part to play in controlling the climate. Until recently people saw these oceans as being so big that there was nothing they could do that would have an effect on them, but after decades of pollution and over-fishing, we are learning that there is a limit to the way in which we can treat them.

In the natural course of events, storm-driven wave action will occasionally damage coral reefs, but some human activities, such as blast and cyanide fishing, coral mining, landfilling, siltation caused by dredging or logging, and the indiscriminate collection of corals to sell as marine curios, are just as destructive. Over-fishing depletes fish life, upsets the food chain and, in the case of herbivorous fish, can lead to the corals in an area becoming overgrown with algae.

Environmentalists are increasingly concerned by the damage done by a few divers to live corals. Some dive operators in warm waters have banned the use of gloves, except on wrecks, in an effort to stop divers from holding on to corals. If divers have to settle on the seabed to practise diving exercises or adjust their equipment, they should do so only on areas of dead sand so that they do not kill any live coral or other marine creatures.

The growing awareness of environmental issues has given rise to ecotourism — tourism with an ecological conscience.

A SOFT TREE CORAL AND GORGONIAN FAN ARE BACKLIT BY SUNLIGHT FILTERING THROUGH THE WATER. PRESERVING DELICATE REEF SYSTEMS IS A WORLDWIDE CHALLENGE FOR DIVERS.

much-needed employment and income becomes available for the local population. In the long term, the profits derived from ecotourism generally exceed those of logging or over-fishing.

Although many divers, dive operators and diving resorts have been at the forefront of efforts to

Ecotourism is often termed 'take nothing but photographs, leave nothing but footprints' but in the sea even footprints, like any form of touching, can be a problem for corals. A better description of ecotourism is managing tourism and tourists in such a way as to be ecologically sustainable. While the capital investment necessary to develop ecotourism is often minimal,

protect reefs and marine ecosystems, we all need some-where to eat and sleep. If one small resort is built without proper waste treatment systems, the nearby reefs may not be irreparably damaged. However, if those same reefs begin to attract increasing numbers of divers and spawn further resorts, then strict controls become necessary, not only applicable at the resorts themselves, but also to visiting divers from nearby areas and visiting live-aboard boats.

Coral reefs are not the only places where divers have an effect on local ecosystems, but the more popular reefs are where the largest concentration of divers can be found. There is also concern over the behaviour of some divers where annual congregations of larger animals occur, but this can be controlled by educating divers and dive operators. Keeping popular areas of the marine environment ecologically sustainable depends as much on divers as it does on the dive operators and resorts.

Basic Guidelines

■ Do not touch living marine animals or organisms either with your body or your equipment.

■ Be particularly careful to control your fins, as their size and the force produced by the fin-stroke can damage large areas of coral. Do not use deep fin-strokes near the reef, as the surge of water can disturb delicate organisms.

■ Master buoyancy control — too much damage is caused by divers descending too rapidly or crashing into corals while trying to adjust their buoyancy. Be properly weighted and, if you have not dived for a while, practise your skills in an area where you will not cause any damage.

■ Do not kick up sand. Clouds of sand settling on the reef can smother corals. Snorkellers should also be careful not to kick up sand when treading water in shallow reef areas.

■ Do not stand on corals, or pose for pictures inside giant basket or barrel sponges, as living coral polyps are easily damaged by the slightest touch.

■ If you are out of control and about to collide with the reef, steady yourself with your finger-tips on a part of the reef that is already dead or covered in algae. If you need to adjust your diving equipment or mask, do so in a sandy area away from the reef.

■ Do not collect or buy shells, corals, starfish, turtle shells or any other marine souvenirs.

■ On any offshore excursion, whether with an operator or privately organized, make sure you take your garbage back for proper disposal on land.

■ Take care in underwater caverns and caves. Avoid lots of people crowding into the cave, and do not stay too long as your air bubbles collect in the pockets on the roof of the cave and the delicate creatures living there can 'drown' in air.

■ If booking a live-aboard dive trip, ask about the company's environmental policies — particu-larly regarding anchorage and the discharge of sewage. Avoid boats

that cause unnecessary anchor damage, have bad oil leaks, or discharge untreated sewage or waste water near reefs.

■ Do not participate in spear-fishing for sport. Selectively killing the larger fish upsets the chain of reproduction. If you are living on a boat and relying on spear-fishing for food, make sure you are familiar with all local fish and game regulations and obtain any necessary licences.

■ Do not move marine organisms around to photograph or play with them. In particular, do not hitch rides on turtles, manta rays or whale sharks, as it causes them considerable stress.

■ There are two schools of thought on deliberate fish feeding. Most conservationists say do not feed fish. It may seem harmless but it can upset their normal feeding patterns, provoke aggressive behaviour and be unhealthy for them if they are given food that is not part of their normal diet. However, others say that selected feeding of some sharks, dolphins, giant groupers and stingrays has produced themed dives that have had the beneficial effect of making these animals worth more as live diving attractions than they would be if they were dead. This valuable 'advertising' helps to conserve animals that would otherwise be fished out.

The Science of Diving

a ll divers must understand how water and gas pressures affect the human body, in order for the sport to be safe. Some of the laws may initially sound complicated, but they are actually quite straightforward.

We are used to living in air and when we venture underwater our perception of weight, colour, distance, size and sound are different. Water quickly conducts heat away from our bodies, and the pressure at depth acting on the gases we are breathing, the blood and tissues carrying these gases, and the air spaces within the body all have physiological effects on the diver.

Water

Water is made up of two atoms of hydrogen attached to a single atom of oxygen (H_2O). At normal temperatures and pressures water is a liquid, and within the pressure ranges involved in diving, liquids can be considered as incompressible. Water is unusual in that its density decreases at temperatures below 4°C (39°F), so when it freezes, ice actually floats on the surface of water instead of sinking.

Buoyancy

Archimedes' principle states that 'any object that is wholly or partially immersed in a liquid is buoyed up by a force equal to the weight of the liquid displaced by that object'. Put simply, if an object is less dense than the liquid it is in, it will float (positive buoyancy), and if it is denser, it will sink (negative buoyancy).

The diver can increase his or her total weight by using lead weights, while volume can be adjusted in a small way by how deeply he or she breathes and in a larger way by varying the amount of air in a buoyancy compensator device (BCD) until the diver's overall density is the same as that of the surrounding water. At this point the diver becomes neutrally buoyant. (Refer to weight belts p35 and BCDs p36.)

The more dense the liquid, the more buoyant it will be. Salt water contains salts in solution, which makes it denser than fresh water and therefore more buoyant.

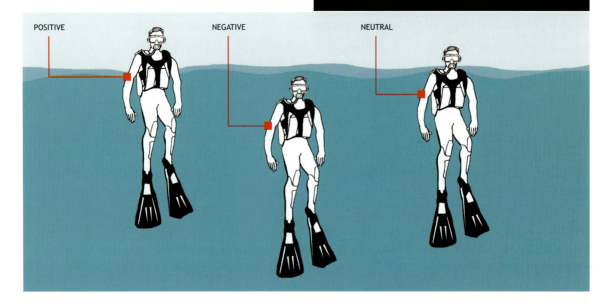

right GOOD BUOYANCY ENABLES DIVERS TO KEEP CLEAR OF THE REEF.

below FINDING AND MAINTAINING THE RIGHT BUOYANCY IS A QUESTION OF WEIGHT AND BREATH CONTROL, AND TAKES TIME TO LEARN.

POSITIVE   NEGATIVE   NEUTRAL

Air

MOST SPORT DIVERS BREATHE compressed air, a mixture of colourless, odourless and tasteless gases. The composition of air in the atmosphere is approximately 78% nitrogen, 21% oxygen and 1% other gases.

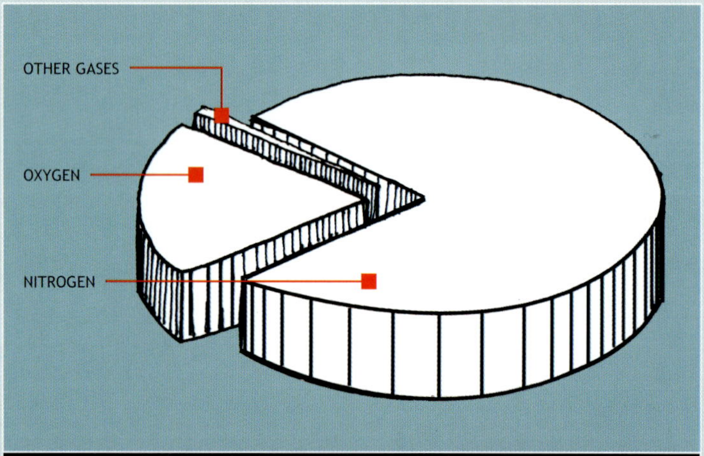

bubbles that become too large for the body to release safely. These bubbles can block blood vessels or tissues, causing decompression sickness (refer to p27). If bubbles block the flow of blood to the brain or heart,

Carbon Dioxide, a major constituent of exhaled air, is produced as a byproduct when food and oxygen are converted into energy. Sensors within our bodies measure the amount of carbon dioxide present as it builds up in our blood and respiratory system, and when the quantity becomes too high, these sensors send signals to the brain which tell it either to commence breathing or to breathe more quickly.

OTHER GASES

OXYGEN

NITROGEN

THIS DIAGRAM SHOWS THE COMPOSITION OF THE AIR WE BREATHE.

Carbon Monoxide, which is formed by incomplete combustion, is highly poisonous as it combines with the haemoglobin in the blood in preference to oxygen. Once haemoglobin is combined with carbon monoxide, it can no longer carry the oxygen we require for life. Divers are at risk as it can enter scuba cylinders through bad compressor maintenance or by locating the compressor air intake in a position where it can pick up exhaust fumes from passing vehicles or other internal combustion engines.

Nitrogen is the major component of air but the body cannot make use of it during breathing. Under the increased pressure of diving, more nitrogen than normal dissolves in the blood and tissues. If we dive deeply enough it interferes with the central nervous system, causing nitrogen narcosis (the effects of which resemble drunkenness). This extra dissolved nitrogen is released from solution in the blood and tissues as the diver ascends. If the diver ascends too quickly, nitrogen is released too rapidly and can form

then permanent injury, even death, are possible.

Oxygen is required to convert food into energy. However, under enough pressure oxygen becomes toxic and the resulting convulsions are particularly dangerous underwater. Many advanced divers now breathe Enriched Air Nitrox (EAN) — the term for air that has been enriched with extra oxygen to reduce the nitrogen content and therefore reduce nitrogen narcosis and the risk of decompression sickness (refer to Enriched Air Nitrox p92).

Helium is an odourless inert (unreactive) gas that is used in place of nitrogen in deep diving to avoid the narcotic effect of nitrogen. However, it distorts the voice, conducts heat away from the body quickly and requires complicated decompression schedules.

The gas laws

Gases are substances that either expand to fill all the space available to them or can be compressed into a smaller volume. In order to understand the behaviour of gases underwater, divers must have some knowledge of the gas laws.

Boyle's law

So long as the temperature remains constant, the pressure is inversely proportional to the volume.

In simple terms, Boyle's law means that as the pressure on a gas increases, the volume of the gas decreases, and vice versa. Another way of explaining Boyle's law is that for a fixed quantity of gas, so long as the temperature does not change, then the pressure multiplied by the volume remains constant.

$P \times V = K$

(where P = absolute pressure, V = volume, K = constant)

If P and V vary $P_1 \times V_1 = K$

And $P_2 \times V_2$ also $= K$

So combining the two equations gives:

$$P_1 \times V_1 = P_2 \times V_2$$

If a fixed quantity of gas is pumped into a rigid container (such as an air cylinder), the volume of that cylinder cannot change so it will determine the pressure of the gas inside. However, if the same quantity of gas is pumped into a flexible container (such as a balloon), the container will expand to keep the pressure inside the container equal to the pressure of the gas or liquid outside the container. In this situation the pressure determines the volume of the container.

At sea level the atmosphere exerts a pressure of 1 bar (14.7psi). At 10m (33ft) below the surface of the water, this pressure is doubled to 2 bar (29.4psi) and for each further 10m (33ft) in depth, the pressure is increased by 1 bar (14.7psi).

Imagine an inverted open bottle, which is full of air, at the surface. At a depth of 10m (33ft), where the pressure is 2 bar (29.4psi), the air in this bottle will have been compressed into half of its original volume.

At 20m (66ft) the pressure will be 3 bar (44.1psi) and the air in the bottle will have been compressed into a third of its original volume. At 30m (100ft) the pressure will be 4 bar (58.8psi) and the air in the bottle will have been compressed into a quarter of its original volume. If the bottle is raised, the reverse occurs and the air in the bottle expands in relation to the reduction in pressure.

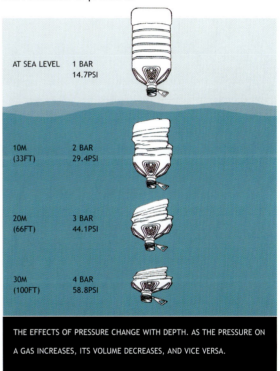

AT SEA LEVEL	1 BAR	14.7PSI
10M (33FT)	2 BAR	29.4PSI
20M (66FT)	3 BAR	44.1PSI
30M (100FT)	4 BAR	58.8PSI

THE EFFECTS OF PRESSURE CHANGE WITH DEPTH. AS THE PRESSURE ON A GAS INCREASES, ITS VOLUME DECREASES, AND VICE VERSA.

While the pressure and volume of a gas are inversely proportional, the pressure and density of a gas are directly proportional. Therefore when we increase the pressure, the volume of a gas is reduced; the space between its molecules is reduced and the gas becomes denser. At twice the atmospheric pressure, a given volume of gas is twice as dense as it would have been at the surface and so on. This explains why divers use up their scuba cylinder's air supply more quickly at depth. A full breath of air at twice atmospheric pressure takes in twice as many air molecules from the cylinder as it would have done at the surface. Therefore, at three atmospheres, a cylinder will only last a third as long as it would have done at the surface.

Charles' law

If a fixed mass of gas is kept at a constant pressure, then the volume is directly proportional to the absolute temperature. (That is, if the temperature is increased, then the volume will also increase.)

PARTICULAR CARE MUST BE TAKEN WHEN FILLING SCUBA TANKS TO ENSURE THAT THE PURITY OF THE AIR IS MAINTAINED AT ALL TIMES AND THAT NO CONTAMINATION OCCURS.

A diver must breathe air at a pressure equal to that of the surrounding water. As this pressure increases with depth, divers breathe through a system of valves, known as a diving regulator, that reduces the pressure of the compressed air in the scuba cylinder to a pressure equal to that of the water at the same depth as the diver's lungs. Once underwater, divers do not wish to waste the air in their cylinder, so the modern diving regulator has been designed to only supply air when demanded, hence the frequently used alternative name 'demand valve' (refer to diving regulators p44).

On every dive we have several gas-filled containers, such as the devices used to control buoyancy (e.g. BCDs), scuba cylinders, masks and even small bubbles in wet and neoprene dry suits. Within the body there are also gas-filled cavities such as the sinuses, ears, stomach and lungs (refer to p29).

Except for rigid scuba cylinders, all these gas-filled spaces continuously contract as we descend and expand as we ascend.

When ascending, divers must make sure that they breathe out frequently enough to get rid of the air expanding in their lungs and must also remember to equalize their ears and sinuses, in order to avoid tissue damage, or barotrauma (refer to p28).

Current thinking is that the rate at which gases expand within a diver's body during ascent is particularly high in the top 10m (33ft) of the dive, so divers should forcibly breathe out, while ascending very slowly, from a depth of 10m to the surface.

The constant volume law

If the volume of a fixed mass of gas is kept constant, then the pressure is directly proportional to the temperature.

Dalton's law

In a mixture of gases, the pressure exerted by any one of the gases is the same as it would exert if it alone occupied the same volume.

If the temperature is increased, so is the pressure. Similarly, if the pressure is increased, so is the temperature. This is the reason why full scuba cylinders, which have a constant volume, should not be stored near to a source of heat or in direct sunlight, as the expanding gas could cause them to explode.

As a rule of thumb, for every 1°C of temperature change, the pressure in a full diving cylinder will change by 0.6 bar. For 1°F of temperature change, the pressure in a full diving cylinder will change by 5psi.

Boyle's law, Charles' law and the constant volume law can be combined as:

$$\frac{P \times V}{T} = K$$

Where P = absolute pressure; V = volume; T = absolute temperature; K = constant.
This gives the mathematical equation:

$$\frac{P_1 \times V_1}{T_1} = K$$

But if things vary then:

$$\frac{P_2 \times V_2}{T_2} \text{ is also} = K$$

Combining the two equations gives a mathematical equation for the general gas law:

$$\frac{P_1 \times V_1}{T_1} = \frac{P_2 \times V_2}{T_2}$$

When filling or emptying a diving cylinder both V_1 and V_2 are identical, so they cancel each other out and the equation becomes:

$$\frac{P_1}{T_1} = \frac{P_2}{T_2}$$

In practice it is impossible to avoid altering all three parameters together. For example, when a diving cylinder is filled from a compressor, the air is heated by the compressor and then warms the diving cylinder.

Thus the total pressure exerted by a mixture of gases is equal to the sum of the pressures of each of the gases making up the mixture. Put simply, each individual gas within a mixture of gases acts independently of the other gases. When gases are mixed, although their molecules vary in size and molecular weight, they are in constant motion so they will mix easily. In a mixture of gases, each gas exerts a pressure proportional to the percentage of that gas in the total. The individual pressure exerted by an individual gas within a mixture of gases is referred to as the partial pressure (pp).

For example, if we assume that air is made up of four-fifths nitrogen and one-fifth oxygen, then the nitrogen molecules will exert four-fifths of the pressure and the oxygen molecules will exert one-fifth of the pressure. If the total pressure is one atmosphere then the partial pressure of the nitrogen will be four-fifths of an atmosphere and the partial pressure of oxygen will be one-fifth of an atmosphere.
Mathematically Dalton's law can be expressed as:

TOTAL P = ppA + ppB + ppC etc.

or ppA = TOTAL P x % volume A

where A, B and C are the individual gases in the mixture.

As the diver descends, the pressure of the water at the same depth as his or her lungs increases, as does the pressure inside the lungs. The lungs are flexible, so to maintain their original volume, they take in more gas through the regulator.

While individual percentages within a gas mixture remain constant, the number of gas molecules within a given volume increase with the pressure. This means that we take in considerably more of the individual gases with each breath at depth than we would normally do at the surface. Taken in enough quantity, even normally safe gases such as oxygen become toxic. If a poorly sited compressor is used to fill a diving cylinder with 0.5% by volume of carbon monoxide, we would not taste or smell it at the surface and are unlikely to suffer more than a headache by breathing it. However, if the diver descends to 40m (132ft), the partial pressure of the carbon monoxide will have increased enough to be the equivalent of breathing 2.5 per cent by volume of the gas at the surface — a toxic level.

Enriched Air Nitrox and Dalton's law

Nowadays many divers breathe Enriched Air Nitrox (EAN) — where extra oxygen has been added to replace some of the nitrogen (refer to EAN diving p 92). When compared with a diver breathing normal air, divers breathing Enriched Air Nitrox absorb less nitrogen for a given depth and duration, so they have a longer no-decompression time or a shorter decompression time.

However, above a partial pressure of 1.4ata (atmospheres absolute), oxygen toxicity becomes unacceptable. When diving on normal air, this partial pressure of oxygen would only occur when diving deeper than sport-diving depths, but with Enriched Air Nitrox it occurs within those depths. Divers must observe depth limits according to the percentage of oxygen in the mix.

Henry's law

This law involves the absorption of gases by liquids. At a given temperature, the amount of gas that will dissolve in a liquid with which it is in contact is proportional to the partial pressure of that gas.

Thus there are at least two factors that affect the solubility of gas in a liquid — pressure and temperature. The spaces between the molecules in a liquid are greater than those in a solid, but less than those in a gas. There is enough room between the molecules of a liquid to accommodate some gas molecules. When this happens, the gas is in solution (dissolved within the liquid). Gas molecules in solution retain their gas properties. Although they are completely surrounded by the liquid molecules, the gas molecules still exert a pressure within the liquid; this is known as 'gas tension'.

Let us use the example of a container of liquid that initially has no gas dissolved in it. In this state the gas tension is zero. Gas molecules flow from high to low pressure, therefore if this liquid comes into contact with a gas, the gas molecules will penetrate into the liquid because it has a lower gas tension. If gas continues to enter the liquid, the gas tension will continue to rise until the gas pressure within the liquid is equal to the pressure of the gas in contact with the liquid. The liquid is then saturated and gas molecules will continue to pass into and out of solution, but there will be no net exchange of gas.

The difference between the partial pressure of the gas in contact with the liquid and the gas tension within the liquid is called the pressure gradient. When the pressure gradient is high, the rate of absorption of the gas into the liquid will be high.

If the pressure on the gas in contact with the liquid is reduced, the pressure gradient is reversed. The liquid is now supersaturated (that is, it contains more gas than it can retain in solution at the new pressure). Consequently gases will flow out of solution until the gas tension within the liquid is again in equilibrium with the pressure of the gases in contact with it.

If the pressure is reduced quickly, the gas will come out of solution more rapidly than it can diffuse into the gas in contact with the liquid. In this situation the gas will form bubbles. This can be observed when we remove the sealing cap from an aerated (fizzy) drink bottle, allowing bubbles of carbon dioxide to escape from solution.

As far as the human body is concerned, when we dive to various depths, different tissues absorb or release nitrogen at different rates. This is also dependent on other variables such as the blood circulation, temperature and the amount of exercise performed.

So long as the diver has ascended slowly enough, when he or she returns to the surface the body will continue to slowly release nitrogen in a safe manner. However, if the diver has not ascended correctly, then nitrogen may be given off so quickly that large enough bubbles are formed in the tissues to result in decompression sickness (refer to p 27).

Systems of measurement

MOST COUNTRIES BASE THEIR measurements on the metric system (metres, kilograms, litres, etc.). This is easy to use because it is based on units of 10. Some countries still use the imperial system (feet, pounds, pints, etc.). Measurements in feet are useful as 12 is divisible by 2, 3, 4 and 6 whereas 10 is only divisible by 2 and 5.

One kilogram (1kg) is the weight of one litre of water (approximately 2.2 lb).

One metre is derived from the speed of light in a vacuum and equals 39.37in.

Pressure can be expressed in kilograms per square centimetre (kg/cm^2), pounds per square inch (psi) or millimetres of mercury (mmHg).

The atmosphere (the air in which we normally live) has its own weight, pressing equally on us in all directions and on the ground as pressure.

At average sea level this pressure, called barometric pressure, or one atmosphere, is universally accepted to be 760mmHg or 14.7psi at 0°C (32°F). In the metric system this is usually referred to as 1 bar.

Atmospheric (barometric) pressure varies with changes in weather conditions and decreases with altitude.

Most pressure gauges read zero at sea level, although they should be reading the pressure of the atmosphere. This leads to a difference in the way that true pressure is measured. If a gauge reads 200 bar (2940psi), it really means 200 bars above atmospheric pressure. This is known as gauge pressure and is signified by a 'g' after the unit measurement (for example, 1 bar gauge or 14.7psig).

In reality, if the gauge was calibrated to true zero, such as found in a vacuum, it would read 201 bar (2955psi), the extra pressure being the atmospheric pressure. Such a reading is referred to as absolute pressure and is signified by adding an 'a' at the end of the unit of measurement (for example, 1 bar absolute or 14.7psia). If measuring in atmospheres we use ata for atmospheres absolute.

Depth gauges read pressure, and are only accurate when used in the environment for which they are calibrated. Those calibrated for sea water will not be accurate in fresh water; those zeroed for sea level will not read accurately at altitude.

For measuring temperature, the metric system uses degrees Celsius (°C) and the imperial system uses degrees Fahrenheit (°F). Both systems are based on the freezing point (0°C or 32°F) and the boiling point (100°C or 212°F) of pure water.

To convert from Celsius to Fahrenheit, multiply the Celsius figure by 9, divide by 5, and add 32: $(°C \times 9 \div 5) + 32 = °F$. To convert from Fahrenheit to Celsius, subtract 32 from the Fahrenheit figure, multiply the result by 5, and divide by 9: $(°F - 32) \times 5 \div 9 = °C$.

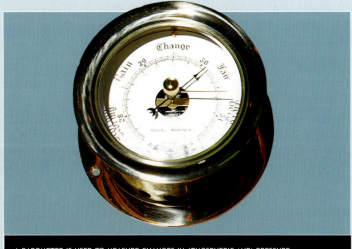

A BAROMETER IS USED TO MEASURE CHANGES IN ATMOSPHERIC (AIR) PRESSURE.

Diving & the Body

Scuba equipment allows us to breathe underwater. Regulators increase the resistance to our breathing workload, however, and this gets progressively larger as we descend, with increased external pressures on the lungs causing greater resistance to their expansion and making the breathing gases denser. In the same way as athletes become fitter by training, divers adapt by regular diving. Oxygen consumption is reduced as the body learns to use oxygen more efficiently and a greater tolerance to carbon dioxide build-up develops.

The cardiovascular system

The circulatory and respiratory systems (the cardiovascular system) provide oxygen and nutrients to the body and remove carbon dioxide. In the body, food is converted into carbohydrates, which react chemically with oxygen and change into energy, water and carbon dioxide.

If body tissues do not receive enough oxygen (O_2) they may die (hypoxia). To maintain the necessary levels of oxygen and carbon dioxide (CO_2) in the blood, the brain regulates breathing according to changes in the blood's carbon dioxide content. Normal breathing occurs when the brain detects a build-up of carbon dioxide. However unconsciousness can occur if one hyperventilates after a breath-hold dive, when the respiratory centre is not stimulated because the carbon dioxide level has been lowered and the brain fails to respond properly to the fall in oxygen level. The tissues of the brain and nervous system consume nearly one-fifth of the oxygen transported by the circulatory system. If these tissues are deprived of oxygen they begin to die within minutes, whereas other body tissues can survive for hours without oxygen.

During exercise, or when the body is under stress, the rate and pressure of circulation increases, so that more oxygen can be supplied to the tissues and more carbon dioxide removed. The pressure and volume of the blood supply must not drop so low as to starve tissues of oxygen or rise so high as to rupture arteries.

Know your heart

The body reacts to fright or stress by releasing adrenaline into the blood system to stimulate the heart and the breathing rate, and constrict blood vessels in preparation for fighting or fleeing. Both stress and moderate exercise occur during recreational diving so persons with a history of cardiac problems or high blood pressure should consult a doctor specializing in diving, before participating in the sport.

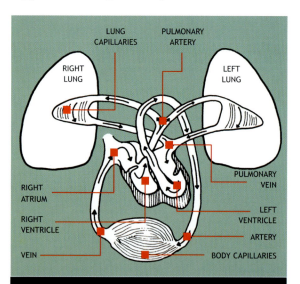

above OXYGENATED BLOOD FROM THE LUNGS ENTERS THE LEFT SIDE OF THE HEART AND IS THEN PUMPED THROUGH ARTERIES, WHICH BRANCH INTO SMALLER ARTERIES AND FINALLY INTO TINY BLOOD VESSELS CALLED CAPILLARIES. IN THE CAPILLARIES, THE BLOOD EXCHANGES OXYGEN FOR CARBON DIOXIDE AND THEN RETURNS TO THE LUNGS THROUGH THE VEINS. BACK IN THE LUNGS THE BLOOD RELEASES ITS CARBON DIOXIDE, TAKES IN FRESH OXYGEN AND BEGINS ANOTHER CYCLE.
right UNDERSTANDING HOW THE BODY RESPONDS TO PRESSURE AND TEMPERATURE CHANGES MAKES DIVING SAFER AND MORE PLEASURABLE.

Hypercapnia (also called hypercarbia)

This is an excess of carbon dioxide. It can have several causes but it is most commonly due to heavy physical exertion and inadequate ventilation of the lungs. Under heavy exertion, the muscle tissues produce carbon dioxide faster than the respiratory system can release it. The high levels of carbon dioxide stimulate faster breathing, producing even more carbon dioxide and creating a vicious circle that only ceases when the diver stops all activity and allows breathing to return to normal. When we exhale, the last portion of gas breathed out of our lungs only gets as far as the large airways. It is not cleared but breathed back in with the next breath; we call the passages containing this gas 'dead space'. If this dead space is not being ventilated properly, we could suffer from hypercapnia. Carbon dioxide contamination and skip-breathing (holding one's breath in an attempt to increase bottom time or to approach skittish subjects quietly), can also cause hypercapnia. Usually there is a headache, mental confusion and dizziness, but hypercapnia can also cause unconsciousness.

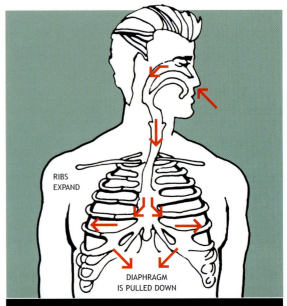

RIBS EXPAND

DIAPHRAGM IS PULLED DOWN

INSPIRATION: WHEN BREATHING IN, THE CHEST WALL IS PULLED OUT BY THE CHEST-WALL MUSCLES AND THE DIAPHRAGM IS PULLED DOWN. THUS THE PRESSURE WITHIN THE CHEST AND LUNGS IS REDUCED AND AIR FLOWS INTO THE LUNGS.

Hypocapnia (also called hypocarbia)

This is the reverse of hypercapnia, and results from too little carbon dioxide. It is mostly caused by hyper-ventilation (either voluntary or involuntary) due to fright or stress. As carbon dioxide is not allowed to build up, the brain does not sense the need to breathe and the diver's oxygen level may fall below the level required to remain conscious. At depth the increased partial pressure of oxygen in the lungs (see p 19) allows the body to continue consuming oxygen even after it has dropped below the level that would cause unconsciousness at the surface. As the diver ascends, the partial pressure of oxygen in the lungs falls below the level at which it can bond with haemoglobin. The result is hypoxia (lack of oxygen) and the diver blacks out. This is termed shallow-water blackout or hypoxia of ascent.

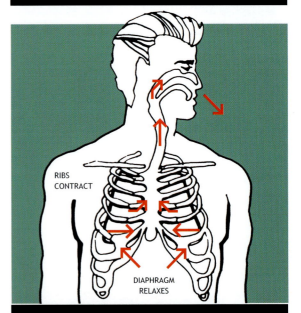

RIBS CONTRACT

DIAPHRAGM RELAXES

EXHALATION: BREATHING OUT IS MOSTLY DUE TO THE ELASTIC RECOIL OF THE LUNGS AND CHEST WALL AFTER EXPANSION. THIS INCREASES THE PRESSURE WITHIN THE CHEST AND FORCES EXHALED AIR OUT FROM THE LUNGS. NO MUSCULAR EFFORT IS INVOLVED UNLESS THE DIVER EXHALES FORCEFULLY.

Carbon monoxide poisoning

Carbon monoxide bonds with haemoglobin in the blood 200 times more readily than with oxygen. Therefore where both carbon monoxide and oxygen are present, the carbon monoxide will bond with the haemoglobin in preference to the oxygen, and these bonds are not easily broken. It can take 8–12 hours of breathing clean air before all carbon monoxide is eliminated. When haemoglobin is carrying carbon monoxide it cannot carry oxygen, so if carbon monoxide poisoning goes unnoticed, hypoxia can result.

When diving at depth, the increased pressure enables enough oxygen to dissolve in the plasma to support the body's needs, delaying the onset of warning symptoms such as a headache, confusion or narrowed vision. As the diver ascends, there is no longer enough pressure to dissolve sufficient oxygen in the plasma and the diver blacks out (hypoxia of ascent).

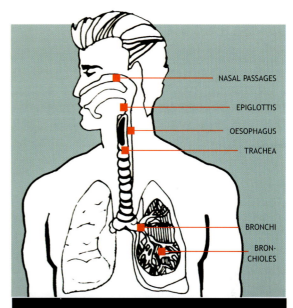

NASAL PASSAGES

EPIGLOTTIS

OESOPHAGUS

TRACHEA

BRONCHI

BRON-CHIOLES

BREATHING AND THE LUNGS: WHEN WE BREATHE IN, AIR FLOWS THROUGH THE MOUTH, NOSE AND SINUSES, PAST THE EPIGLOTTIS (A FLAP OF SKIN THAT STOPS FOOD FROM ENTERING THE WINDPIPE), AND INTO THE WINDPIPE (TRACHEA). THIS BRANCHES INTO LEFT AND RIGHT PASSAGES (THE BRONCHI) AND EACH OF THESE BRONCHI DIVIDES MANY TIMES TO PRODUCE MANY TINY BRONCHIOLES (SMALLER PASSAGES). EACH BRONCHIOLE ENDS IN AN AIR SAC (ALVEOLI); THESE ARE FILLED WITH CAPILLARIES WHERE THE GASES CAN EASILY DIFFUSE ACROSS THE THIN WALLS INTO OR OUT OF THE BLOOD.

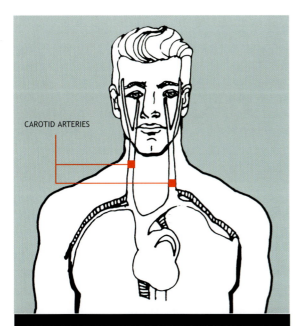

CAROTID ARTERIES

CAROTID-SINUS REFLEX: WHEN THE CAROTID-SINUS SENSOR DETECTS HIGH BLOOD PRESSURE, IT TELLS THE BRAIN TO SLOW DOWN THE HEART RATE. IF THE DIVER HAS AN OVER-TIGHT DRY SUIT NECK SEAL, WET SUIT HOOD OR OTHER EQUIPMENT THAT PRESSES ON THE NECK, THE CAROTID-SINUS SENSORS MAY MISTAKENLY INTERPRET THIS EXCESS PRESSURE AS HIGH BLOOD PRESSURE AND CAUSE THE HEART TO SLOW DOWN, CAUSING UNCONSCIOUSNESS.

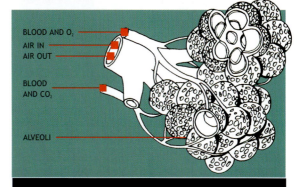

BLOOD AND O₂

AIR IN

AIR OUT

BLOOD AND CO₂

ALVEOLI

THE LUNGS: THESE RESEMBLE TWO LARGE SPONGES, BUT DESPITE THE HUGE AREA AVAILABLE FOR GAS DIFFUSION THE LUNGS ONLY ABSORB A SMALL PERCENTAGE OF THE OXYGEN (O_2) AVAILABLE IN EACH BREATH. A LARGE PERCENTAGE OF OXYGEN REMAINS IN EXHALED BREATH, WHICH EXPLAINS WHY EXHALED AIR RESUSCITATION (ALSO KNOWN AS MOUTH-TO-MOUTH, REFER TO P 78) CONTAINS ENOUGH OXYGEN TO SUSTAIN LIFE.

Oxygen toxicity

When exercising heavily under pressure we build up carbon dioxide in the bloodstream, causing the haemoglobin to give up oxygen more quickly, resulting in the increased exposure of the brain to high oxygen levels (oxygen toxicity or poisoning). The build-up of carbon dioxide also signals to the brain that we should breathe faster, so energetic dives should not be performed on breathing mixtures high in oxygen.

As with nitrogen, the length of time we are exposed to high partial pressures of oxygen has a cumulative effect. This is not a concern in normal recreational diving, but for deep diving, diving on enriched air, or during recompression treatment, we must monitor the 'oxygen clock' and allow sensible surface intervals.

There are two types of oxygen toxicity. Low-dosage, long-term pulmonary or whole-body toxicity (the Lorraine Smith effect) produces symptoms similar to pneumonia, but requires longer exposures to oxygen than recreational divers normally experience. High-dosage, short-term or central nervous system toxicity (the Paul Bert effect) becomes a risk with oxygen above a partial pressure of 1.4ata (atmospheres absolute), (refer to pp 19 and 92). When diving on Enriched Air Nitrox, we reach the 1.4ata limit within recreational diving depths, so detailed training is essential for this type of diving (refer to p 92).

Symptoms of oxygen toxicity are unconsciousness or convulsions, both of which would probably lead to drowning if they occurred underwater.

Nitrogen narcosis

When diving, nitrogen is dissolved in the blood and tissues in direct proportion to depth until those tissues are saturated. The uptake or release of nitrogen varies with the type of tissue, body temperature and the rate of circulation of the blood.

Nitrogen dissolves faster in fat than in water, so body tissues high in fat will absorb more than those low in fat. Tissues served by a large blood flow (called fast tissues) will absorb or release nitrogen quickly. Tissues with a poor blood flow (slow tissues), cartilage, tendons and stored body fat will absorb and release nitrogen slowly, although they can hold more dissolved nitrogen than fast tissues. When the diver ascends, the nitrogen in the tissues is released.

Almost any gas can cause a general loss of sensation (anaesthesia) at high partial pressures, although the

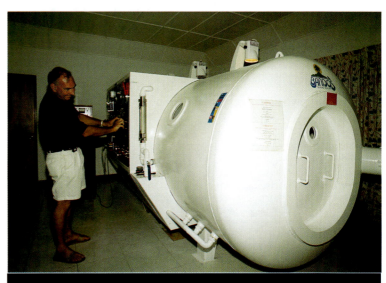

A HYPERBARIC, OR RECOMPRESSION, CHAMBER IS USED TO TREAT DECOMPRESSION SICKNESS.

effect is not uniformly intense. However, it is thought that nitrogen interferes with the electrical transfer from nerve cell to nerve cell, which affects alertness and co-ordination. The result is similar to being drunk, firstly a feeling of elation (also called 'rapture of the deep'), followed by impaired reasoning and a feeling of apprehension. This is known as nitrogen narcosis.

Individuals vary in their susceptibility to nitrogen narcosis. Some divers acclimatize to it with regular exposure, while others learn to cope with it. Some suffer at 30m (100ft) but everyone suffers by 50m (165ft).

Alcohol, tranquillizers, sleeping pills, sea sickness remedies, antihistamines, antidiarrhoeals and any medication that blocks transmission from nerve cells will make things worse or cause narcosis at shallower depths. Nitrogen narcosis may mask the symptoms of other problems and reduce the diver's ability to cope with emergencies. It begins quickly but disappears equally quickly on ascent, and unlike alcohol, there are no after-effects.

Decompression sickness

Decompression sickness (DCS) is caused by dissolved nitrogen being released within the body, instead of being expelled from it. (This is not the same as other decompression-related injuries, which are connected with the lungs expanding too much, but because the treatment for both is the same, they are often referred to together as decompression illness, or DCI.)

The rate that nitrogen is absorbed or released by the body depends on the pressure gradient, the individual's rate of circulation, body temperature and mass of the tissues concerned. After any dive tiny micro-bubbles, which are too small to cause DCS, exist in the tissues and bloodstream. When there are many of these micro-bubbles they combine to form larger ones, and if the pressure gradient is high, bubbles form that are large enough to cause DCS.

When the blood flow is blocked, tissues that are beyond the blockage are starved of oxygen so they become hypoxic and may be permanently damaged. Symptoms depend on the location of the bubbles.

Epidermal or Cutaneous DCS — The skin itches, tingles or exhibits a burning sensation; there may be a patchy red rash. These symptoms often occur almost immediately on leaving the water. They are not dangerous in themselves and disappear quickly, but may be an indication of more serious DCS problems.

Muscular, joint and limb pain DCS — The most commonly reported symptoms of DCS are pains around the large joints (the knees, shoulders and elbows), caused by bubbles forming in or around tendons, ligaments and related muscles. Although the pain may not appear for some hours after a dive, it should be treated seriously. DCS victims often ease the pain by keeping the joint bent and immobile, which has given rise to the term 'the bends' to describe DCS.

Neurological DCS — This occurs when the blood flow to the spinal cord or the brain is restricted. Where the spinal cord is affected there can be numbness, pins-and-needles and paralysis of the lower limbs, difficulty in controlling the bladder or paralysis from the neck down. If the brain is affected there can be blurred vision, headache, confusion, unconsciousness, a stroke and death.

Treatment of decompression sickness — Although a physical injury or a previous incident of DCS makes one more likely to suffer from it, the most common symptom is extreme fatigue. Treat divers with suspected DCS by administering pure oxygen and transport them to the nearest hyperbaric (recompression) chamber. There the patient can be rapidly recompressed to reduce the size of the bubbles and force them back into solution, then decompressed very slowly while being treated with oxygen, given medication (such as drugs to reduce blood clotting) and intravenous fluids. Pure oxygen can cause lung damage when administered continuously, so patients require breaks during which they breathe normal air.

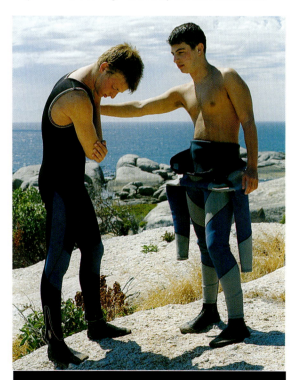

PAINS AROUND THE KNEES, SHOULDERS AND ELBOWS CAN INDICATE THE PRESENCE OF DCS AND SHOULD ALWAYS BE TAKEN SERIOUSLY.

ANY GAS SPACE IN THE BODY can experience barotrauma (pressure injury). Barotraumas of descent are termed 'squeezes' and those of ascent are termed 'reverse squeezes'.

Most of the body is not compressible within recreational diving depths but gases are, so the parts of the body containing gases (the ears, sinuses, teeth, lungs and gastrointestinal tract), as well as the facial area covered by the mask, respond to volume changes that occur when the pressure on the diver changes.

When divers descend their air spaces are squeezed. Divers usually equalize the squeeze on their mask without thinking, but it tends to be more noticeable on rapid descents. Forcibly breathing out through the nose will solve the problem. Similar squeeze on a dry suit can cause pinching and bruising and is solved by adding air to the suit. Make sure that the extra air is released on ascent.

The ears

Normally there are equal pressures on either side of the eardrum. When descending, water pressure forces each eardrum inward causing increased pressure and pain in the middle ear. The middle ear is connected to the throat by the Eustachian tube, so this inner and outer pressure can usually be equalized by swallowing, or by holding the nose closed, closing the mouth and trying to snort out through the nose.

If the Eustachian tubes are congested, usually due to a cold or an allergy, it may be difficult or impossible to equalize. If a diver continues to descend without equalization, fluids and blood are forced into the middle ear and eventually the eardrum ruptures, accompanied by pain and a sense of vertigo until the water that has entered the ear warms up.

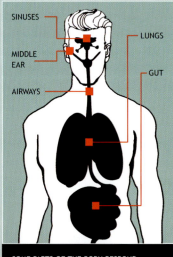

SINUSES

MIDDLE EAR

AIRWAYS

LUNGS

GUT

SOME PARTS OF THE BODY RESPOND AUTOMATICALLY TO CHANGES IN PRESSURE.

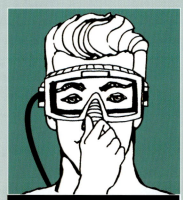

TO EQUALIZE THE PRESSURES ON EITHER SIDE OF THE EARDRUM, HOLD THE NOSE, SHUT THE MOUTH AND TRY TO SNORT THROUGH THE NOSE. THIS SHOULD OPEN THE EUSTACHIAN TUBES.

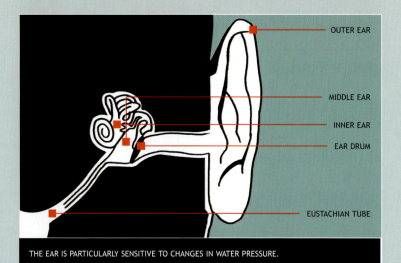

OUTER EAR

MIDDLE EAR

INNER EAR

EAR DRUM

EUSTACHIAN TUBE

THE EAR IS PARTICULARLY SENSITIVE TO CHANGES IN WATER PRESSURE.

When ascending, expanding air usually vents through the Eustachian tubes to the throat without any conscious effort by the diver.

A reverse ear squeeze on ascent often occurs when decongestants that have been taken to facilitate diving with a cold wear off. In this case your air supply dictates how long you can try to equalize before you are forced to the surface. Decongestants are not recommended for diving.

The sinuses

When descending with congestion of the sinuses, water pressure forces blood and fluid into the air cavities and on ascent these fluids are pushed by the expanding air into the nose and usually into the mask.

The teeth

Cavities in teeth due to tooth decay or poor fillings may cause pain as air expands within them on ascent. This is painful but not serious. Consult a dentist.

The lungs

Provided that divers breathe continuously and ascend slowly, they will not have problems with changing pressure in the lungs. The golden rule of diving is 'never hold your breath'. The risk of gases in the lungs over-expanding on ascent is highest in shallow water, so forcibly breathe out while ascending the last 10m (33ft).

Over-expansion causes the lungs to tear. The tears themselves are not serious, but problems arise from air entering the tissues or bloodstream. The most serious problem is air embolism, when enough air enters the pulmonary vein through the torn alveoli to be pumped across the heart to the arterial side, from where bubbles can be pumped around the body and block blood flow.

When a lung has torn, air can escape into the part of the chest containing the windpipe and heart, reducing the efficiency of these organs (mediastinal emphysema) and into the soft tissues at the base of the neck (subcutaneous emphysema). If air gets between the lungs and the chest wall, the outside pressure on the lungs causes them to collapse. The symptoms are chest pain, shortness of breath and frothy blood emitted from the mouth.

While DCS is often delayed, the symptoms of lung injuries occur immediately on surfacing. If circulation to the heart is blocked then the symptoms are those of a heart attack. If the arteries to the central nervous system are obstructed, there could be poor co-ordination, dizziness, paralysis, convulsions, unconsciousness or death.

Not all of these conditions are life threatening, but as they can indicate that a lung has been torn and could lead to air embolism, they should be treated as urgent and the final decisions left to a doctor who is experienced in treating divers and diving-related conditions. In the short term, however, treat as you would for DCS, that is, administer pure oxygen and transport the patient to the nearest hyperbaric (recompression) chamber.

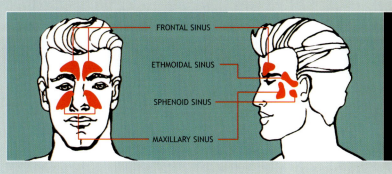

FRONTAL SINUS

ETHMOIDAL SINUS

SPHENOID SINUS

MAXILLARY SINUS

THE SINUSES OF HEALTHY DIVERS ARE AIR-FILLED, MUCOUS-LINED CAVITIES AND TUBES IN THE SKULL THAT NORMALLY EQUALIZE AUTOMATICALLY WHEN EQUALIZING THE EARS. WHENEVER POSSIBLE, AVOID DIVING WITH A COLD, ALLERGY OR NASAL CONGESTION.

Gastrointestinal barotrauma

Abdominal discomfort and colicky pains occur when divers have swallowed compressed gases or recently taken a heavy meal or aerated drink. Apart from avoiding these before a dive, it can help if you descend in an upright position and slow or pause on ascent.

Overexertion

Swimming too hard increases the heart rate and blood pressure, and it may also demand more air from your regulator than it can supply. This produces sensations of suffocation and apprehension, which can lead to panic. Ideally you should stop and allow your breathing and heart rate to return to normal.

Most overexertion involves swimming against a current. If the bottom is free of live coral, you will find it easier to pull yourself along the bottom than to swim.

Hyperthermia

Hyperthermia, or high body temperature, occurs as a result of one or more of the following: exercise, over-insulation, exposure to heat and inadequate fluid intake. Normally, the body sweats to cool down, but exposure suits impede this function and an overheated diver may become incoherent and collapse.

The casualty should be moved to a cool environment and placed under a fan or sponged down with a wet cloth. If the person is conscious, give sweet drinks with half a teaspoon of salt per litre (1.75 European pints or 2 US pints) orally. If the casualty is unconscious, place him or her in the recovery position, monitor the airway, breathing and circulation and seek medical help.

Hypothermia

Optimum body temperature is 36.9°C (98.4°F) plus or minus 0.5°C (0.9°F). If it falls below this a person has hypothermia, or low body temperature.

Ocean temperatures are generally lower than optimum body temperature, so divers require insulation in order to spend prolonged periods in the water. Shivering is an early symptom of the body being too cold, followed by the arms and legs becoming numb as the blood flow to them is restricted. If not treated, incoordination and loss of consciousness can occur.

The treatment is to warm the person up from the outside in. If possible, place the diver in a hot bath

EXPOSURE SUITS CAN INCREASE THE RISK OF HYPERTHERMIA. AFFECTED DIVERS SHOULD BE SPONGED DOWN WITH COLD WATER.

HYPOTHERMIC DIVERS NEED TO WARMED UP WITH BLANKETS AND HOT DRINKS. TOWELS MAY BE USED IF BLANKETS ARE NOT AVAILABLE.

with the legs elevated. Expired air resuscitation (EAR) and cardiopulmonary resuscitation (CPR) may be necessary (refer to EAR p78 and CPR p79).

If the patient is conscious, warm fluids and glucose should be given by mouth but never alcohol, as it increases the blood supply to the extremities and makes the condition worse. Where a hot bath is not possible, the best treatment is to lie other unaffected divers against the patient's skin in as warm and sheltered an environment as can be found, for example, in the shelter of rocks and under blankets.

There is a problem when divers suffering from hypothermia are lifted into a boat or winched up to a rescue helicopter. As the casualty is lifted from the water and the pressure of the water is removed, blood returns to the extremities and gravity forces it down to the legs. The central volume of blood is reduced and the casualty can become shocked and die. These deaths can be avoided by lifting the casualty in the horizontal position with the legs raised.

Near drowning

This describes the situation where fluid has been inhaled into the lungs but death has not occurred. Wet drowning is the term for water entering the lungs. Dry drowning occurs when inhaled water causes the larynx to spasm and the resulting coughing prevents the diver from maintaining an adequate breathing pattern.

Victims will be cyanosed (bluish-purple in colour), not breathing and may have bloodstained froth coming from the mouth and nose. Raise the casualty's legs, give expired air resuscitation (EAR) and cardiopulmonary resuscitation (CPR) and keep going until the casualty recovers or is pronounced dead by a doctor.

Casualties of near drowning have recovered after up to 40 minutes of immersion, especially in cold water, so continue attempting to revive them for at least an hour. If the casualty begins to breathe, then administer pure oxygen where possible.

Damage to the lungs may cause secondary drowning some hours or even days after revival. This can only be treated in hospital, so survivors of near drowning incidents should be admitted to hospital for observation.

With scuba diving accidents, it may be impossible to decide the cause. Fortunately near drowning, lung expansion injuries and DCS all require the same initial treatments: EAR and CPR as required, followed by pure oxygen and transporting the patient as quickly as possible to a hospital with a hyperbaric chamber.

Cramps

Cramps are painful contractions of the muscle brought about by exercise, cold or abnormalities in body salts. Relief is normally obtained by stretching and massaging the muscle. When diving, cramp usually occurs in the calf muscle, so pulling the fin towards the body while straightening the leg should help to ease the pain. If cramps persist, it is advisable to end the dive.

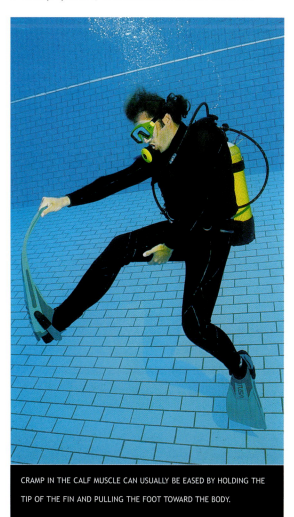

CRAMP IN THE CALF MUSCLE CAN USUALLY BE EASED BY HOLDING THE TIP OF THE FIN AND PULLING THE FOOT TOWARD THE BODY.

Basic equipment

Over the years, diving equipment has become increasingly efficient, more comfortable to wear and more stylish than in the early days of the sport. With the wide variety of equipment readily available, there is no reason why divers should not enter the water properly equipped for the conditions they are diving in. All diving equipment will last longer and be less likely to malfunction if it is kept out of the sun and washed thoroughly with fresh water after use.

Face masks

The human eye cannot focus in water because water has a higher density than air and therefore transmits light in a different way. For clear vision underwater we wear a mask to maintain an air space in front of the eyes.

As this air space is affected by water pressure and may need to be equalized as the diver descends, the diver's nose should be within the mask so that he or she can exhale through the nose into the mask. The nose should also be within a flexible pocket so that the nostrils can be pinched while the diver snorts to facilitate the equalization of ears and sinuses.

A good modern diving mask will have the following features:

■ Silicone rubber skirts, which are comfortable, non-allergenic and maintain flexibility over a wide range of temperatures. Masks can be either translucent or brightly coloured, as long as they allow plenty of light to reach the diver's face. High-quality masks have double-skirts (two skirts around the edges) to give a better seal.

■ A strong retaining strap (head band) with a nonslip adjustment. (It is advisable to always carry a spare mask-retaining strap with your equipment.)

■ Low volume for easy equalization.

■ Tempered glass, which is less easy to break and resists scratches more than plain glass. If it does break it shatters into small, less harmful pieces.

As people's faces and different designs of masks vary considerably in size and shape, you should try several masks for fit and comfort before purchasing. To test a mask, place the retaining strap in front of the face plate out of the way. Look up and fit the mask lightly to your face. Breathe in through your nose. Let go of the mask and shake your head, but be ready to catch the mask should it fall off. Continuing to hold your breath, bend your head down; the mask should remain in place. Check that you can pinch your nose effectively if you need to equalize your ears or sinuses.

RETAINING STRAP

SOFT, FLEXIBLE SKIRT

NON-CORRODING FRAMES

QUICK-RELEASE STRAP ADJUSTMENT

TEMPERED GLASS LENS

NOSE POCKET

above A GOOD DIVING MASK SHOULD HAVE THE FEATURES DESCRIBED.
right DIVERS SHOULD CHOOSE EQUIPMENT SUITED TO THE ENVIRONMENT IN WHICH THEY ARE DIVING. DRY SUITS, AS SHOWN OPPOSITE, SHOULD ALWAYS BE WORN WITH BCDS, AS A SAFETY PRECAUTION.

Can't seal your mask?

Men with moustaches, or people with bone injuries under the upper lip, will never obtain a perfect seal with their mask. Some divers solve this by applying Vaseline (petroleum jelly), but never use this with neoprene rubber masks as it attacks them. With low-volume masks, breathing out regularly through the nose is enough to keep the mask clear of water.

Fins

Fins enable swimmers to move through the water more efficiently. The extra thrust they supply is essential for overcoming the drag of scuba equipment, or when swimming against the current. When wearing fins your hands will be of little help except for minor adjustments of body position or direction.

Fins come in two types:

■ Full foot-pocket fins (used by snorkellers or divers who are not wearing bootees) must be an accurate and comfortable fit. If the heel tears the whole fin has to be replaced, so you must carry spare fins.

■ Open-heel foot-pocket fins are used by divers wearing bootees. The main point of failure with these fins is the adjustable heel strap, so you should always have several spare straps with you.

Fin blades come in various designs and sizes. Larger fins require stronger leg muscles. When choosing fins, fit is more important than design. Fins should not be so tight that they pinch or bruise the foot, nor loose enough to wobble when shaking your feet.

Snorkels

Snorkels allow divers or snorkellers to breathe comfortably on the surface without having to raise their heads out of the water. They allow divers to conserve the air in their scuba cylinder while swimming to a dive site or back to their boat or point of entry when short of air at the end of a dive. Various features make snorkels more comfortable to use and you should select the design that suits you best:

■ Large-bore models with an internal diameter of roughly 25mm (1in) are easiest to breathe through, though smaller-bodied divers may prefer a narrower bore snorkel as it will be easier to clear and will have a smaller mouthpiece.

■ The angle of the mouthpiece must be comfortable in the snorkeller's mouth; some may swivel.

■ Some snorkels have a self-draining barrel or mouthpiece (a one-way valve that allows gravity to drain the portion of the barrel that is clear of the water). There may be an additional valve near the top of the barrel which stops choppy water splashing down it. Even when fitted with both of these valves, water will enter the snorkel, so you should breathe carefully and blow the water out regularly to avoid inhaling it.

When in use the snorkel is attached by a retaining clip to the mask strap or slipped between the mask strap and the diver's head. When not in use the snorkel can be tucked away under the knife straps on the diver's leg.

left (top to bottom) CHOOSE YOUR FINS ACCORDING TO YOUR NEEDS: FORCE FINS OFFER EXTRA EFFICIENCY, AND MAKE FINNING EASIER; THE ADJUSTABLE STRAP OF OPEN-HEEL FOOT-POCKET FINS ENABLES THEM TO FIT OVER BOOTEES; FULL FOOT-POCKET FINS ARE POPULAR WITH SNORKELLERS.
above A SNORKEL IS USEFUL FOR BREATHING ON THE SURFACE WHEN SWIMMING TO A DIVE SITE OR BACK TO THE POINT OF ENTRY.

Weight belts and weights

Most people are positively buoyant in fresh water and this buoyancy increases in denser salt water. Exposure suits, BCDs and nearly-empty scuba cylinders increase buoyancy still further, so to remain submerged divers wear a collection of lead weights on a weight belt.

WEIGHT BELTS AND WEIGHTS ARE USED TO COUNTER POSITIVE BUOYANCY.

If you require several weights the belt can become uncomfortable or unwieldy. Various different weight systems are available, from a plain belt with weights, belts with pockets that will take either standard weights or the more comfortable lead shot, and belts with an additional shoulder harness, to those integrated with a buoyancy control device (BCD).

Whatever system you use it is important that you, or your buddy, are able to 'dump' (release and discard) your weight belt quickly in an emergency without it snagging on any other items of clothing or equipment.

Weight belts are usually made from 5cm-wide (2in) nylon webbing. The quick-release buckle should be a positive fit, easily adjustable and not likely to snag or release when the diver does not want it to.

Weights are usually simple rectangular 1 or 2kg (2 or 4 lb) block mouldings of lead, or cylindrical 'bullet' weights with rounded ends. To prevent the weights moving about on the belt or slipping off, they are held in place with retainers, which may also include a separate ring for a karabiner (snap-link) so that you can attach other items to the belt.

If the weight belt is long enough, block weights can be held in position by passing the belt through one side of the weight and then twisting it over on itself before passing it through the other side.

Weight belts with pockets to take either standard block weights or lead shot are more comfortable and do not allow the weights to move about on the belt.

If your buddy is using an integrated or harness weight system, then you should familiarize yourself with its release mechanism before entering the water.

When flying to an organized diving holiday destination you will not need to pack weights or weight belts, as these will be provided. However, it is wise to carry spare weight retainers.

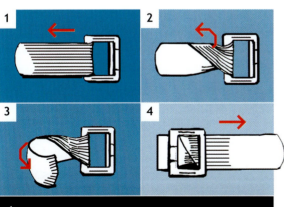

1 TAKE THE LOOSE END OF THE WEIGHT BELT AND THREAD IT THROUGH ONE SIDE OF THE WEIGHT BLOCK.

2 PUT A SINGLE TWIST IN THE BELT.

3 PASS IT BACK THROUGH THE OTHER SIDE OF THE WEIGHT.

4 FINALLY PULL THE BELT TIGHT SO THE WEIGHT IS SECURED FIRMLY IN ONE PLACE.

How much weight?

A properly weighted diver with no air in the BCD, the scuba cylinder less than a quarter full, and carrying any extras that he or she wishes to carry should float in an upright position with the surface at eye level. Less weight will be required if using steel scuba cylinders or diving in fresh water. However more weight will be required with aluminium scuba cylinders (refer to p42).

A BUOYANCY COMPENSATOR device (BCD) enables divers to adjust buoyancy as they descend and ascend, otherwise they will either be constantly finning to stop themselves from sinking or involuntarily float to the surface with possible physiological problems. BCDs contain an air bladder and by adding or dumping air from this, divers can remain neutrally buoyant, enabling them to move more easily underwater, use less air and avoid harmful contact with reef or wreck.

BCDs (also called adjustable buoyancy life jackets or stab jackets) are a multi-component system to which the scuba cylinder, regulator, alternative air supply, accessories and, in some designs, weights, are attached. The whole system can be put on or taken off as a single unit.

Wings (back-mounted inflation BCD) are popular with technical divers and underwater photographers as the air bladder does not cover the front of the body, leaving it free for other equipment or for easier face-down swimming. To achieve good face-up surface flotation with wings, organize a counterweight by having a back-mounted integral weight system, or attach some of the required weight to your scuba cylinder.

The BCD's air bladder system can either be single-bladder, where the bladder itself is both the air container and the cover that takes the wear; or twin-bag, where only the inner bag contains air. Manufactured from polythene, this can be replaced cheaply if damaged. The outer bag is manufactured from a hard-wearing material and is easily

repaired if torn. Twin-bag BCDs are heavier to wear, but more durable and easy to service.

Most BCDs have a low pressure 'direct-feed' or 'power-inflator' connected to the regulator for easy inflation, plus a method of oral inflation. Some are fitted with a carbon dioxide cartridge for one-off emergency inflation at the surface only. Others have an emergency air cylinder with an integral yoke-connector ('A'-clamp) that is filled from a scuba cylinder before each dive.

To rapidly 'dump' (release) air, you pull either a separate cord or a cord enclosed within the corrugated flexible oral-inflation hose to operate a dump valve. Another method is to raise the oral-inflation hose above your head and press the purge button on its end.

above AN INTEGRAL YOKE-CONNECTOR FOR FILLING A BCD EMERGENCY CYLINDER FROM THE MAIN SCUBA CYLINDER.
left A CORRECTLY INFLATED BCD ENABLES A DIVER TO FLOAT MOTIONLESS.

All BCDs have over-pressure release valves in case you over-inflate the bladder or leave the unit inflated out in the sun. These are usually located at the lowest point on the BCD so that if they leak, the bladder will continue to be effective as long as the diver is not constantly head-down. Dump valves should be regularly disas-sembled and any salt or sand flushed away with fresh water to keep them working properly.

Before packing a BCD away, flush out the air bladder with fresh water and thoroughly wash the outside as well. Fill it one-third full through the oral-inflation hose, then shake the jacket around to remove as much saltwater as possible. Drain it in the upside down position with the hose hanging free. Ensure the BCD is quite dry before storing it.

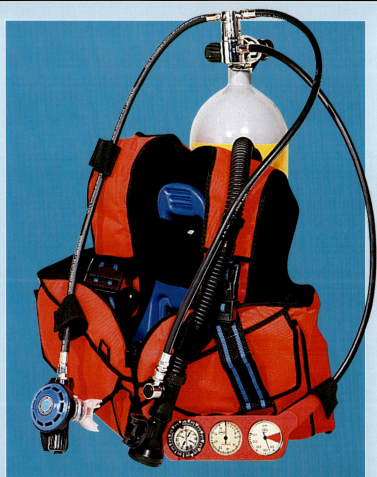

above MOST BCDS HAVE VELCRO-FACED TABS OR RESTRAINING CLIPS TO KEEP REGULATOR HOSES OR INSTRUMENTS CLOSE TO THE BODY WHERE THEY CAN BE READ EASILY AND WILL NOT SNAG ON WRECKS OR MAKE HARMFUL CONTACT WITH THE REEF. MANY ALSO HAVE POCKETS FOR HOLDING SMALLER ITEMS SUCH AS DIVE SLATES AND PENCILS.
left IF YOUR BCD IS TOO SMALL (FAR LEFT) IT WILL NOT SUPPORT YOU ADE-QUATELY, TOO LARGE (LEFT) AND YOUR SCUBA CYLINDER WILL FLOP ABOUT AND HAVE POOR SUPPORT AT THE SURFACE.

YOUR PERSONAL COMFORT level underwater is dictated by your body shape, metabolism, how active you are during a dive, the water temperature and the number of dives that you do during the day. Divers use exposure suits to protect themselves against sunburn at the surface and abrasion, cuts, animal stings and heat loss when in the water. Water conducts heat away from the body considerably faster than air.

Body skins

For very warm water, lightweight one-piece full-body suits (called body skins or Lycra-skins) are often sufficient. Made from nylon with added Lycra to make them highly elastic, they can be brightly coloured and patterned. Unfortunately they deteriorate rapidly in areas of continuously strong sunlight.

Most Lycra body suits have stirrups at the ankles to stop the legs from riding up and loops that slip around the thumbs to keep the arms in place. These are useful for divers who wear body skins for protection or for added insulation under wet suits.

Because of their high elasticity, body skins are sold ready-made in standard sizes.

BRIGHT AND LIGHTWEIGHT, BODY SKINS OFFER THE WARM-WATER DIVER TOTAL FREEDOM OF MOVEMENT.

Wet suits

The commonest form of protection is a wet suit. These are usually made from closed-cell foam neoprene which does not absorb water but provides insulation while having good elasticity.

Wet suits vary in thickness from 2mm (1/16in) for warm water use to 9mm (11/32in) for very cold water. They come in many styles: 'shorties' only cover the upper legs and the torso — the most important area for maintaining heat; whereas one-piece full-body suits provide both thermal and abrasion protection from neck to wrist and ankle.

If you prefer thicker neoprene, two-piece wet suits are popular because they are easier to get into and out of. The most common of these is the 'Farmer John' bottom which covers the body from the ankles to below the shoulders and out again it will be heated by the body and help provide insulation. If the suit is a loose fit, water will flush through it, reducing the suit's thermal effectiveness.

Semi-dry suits have close-fitting neoprene seals at the ankles and wrist. A small amount of water will still enter at the neck but cannot be flushed out through the seals. They can be one- or two-piece and may have a hood attached to the jacket.

is covered by a jacket with a long zip to make it easier to put on and take off. With this system there is a double layer of thermal protection over the torso.

Wet suits should be as tight a fit as is comfortable. Water does enter between the suit and the diver's body but so long as it is not continuously being washed

Wet and semi-dry suit accessories

Accessories for wet or semi-dry suits include hoods (attached or separate), bootees (preferably hard-soled), gloves (nylon for protection against abrasion in warm water or neoprene for warmth in cold water) and spine-pads (an extra layer of neoprene where the natural curve of the spine allows water to flow through). Knee pads protect against abrasion if you kneel on a wreck and help reduce the damage caused by a bent knee stretching the neoprene on the outside of the curve.

above (top to bottom) WET SUITS PROTECT DIVERS FROM SUN AND COLD WATER. HOODS ARE USED IN VERY COLD WATER. NYLON GLOVES PROTECT AGAINST ABRASION. HARD-SOLED BOOTEES ARE EASIER TO WALK IN.

Dry suits

Dry suits fully enclose the body. Where differences exist between makes, these are in the materials used, types of hood and boot, and the position of zips.

Foam neoprene dry suits can be either tight-fitting (like a wet suit) or a looser fit so that they can be worn over warm undergarments. They have inherent insulation properties but lose buoyancy and insulation as the diver descends and the neoprene is compressed.

Membrane (shell) dry suits rely on a waterproof membrane to keep out the water. On their own they do not have any insulation properties and the diver needs to wear warm undergarments.

Most dry suits have built-in boots. Some have built-in hoods while others use a wet suit hood.

Dry suit zips must be kept clean and lubricated with a recommended wax lubricant. The zips are usually positioned across

the shoulders where they will encounter the least bending. There are other positions for zips, such as those that start around the back of the neck and run diagonally down the front, so that a diver can put on the suit without the aid of a buddy.

Dry suit valves

The air in a dry suit is compressed as the diver descends, causing loss of buoyancy and discomfort as creases forming in the material of the suit are squeezed against the body. This can be compensated for by having

left THIS DRY SUIT IS MADE FROM A TRI-LAMINATE OF VULCANIZED RUBBER SANDWICHED BETWEEN TWO LAYERS OF HARD-WEARING SYNTHETIC MATERIAL. AS WITH CRUSHED NEOPRENE THESE SUITS HAVE NO THERMAL INSULATION PROPERTIES OF THEIR OWN BUT RELY ON WARM UNDERGARMENTS.
below THERMAL INSULATION IS ACHIEVED BY DIFFERENT METHODS IN DIFFERENT TYPES OF DIVING SUIT.

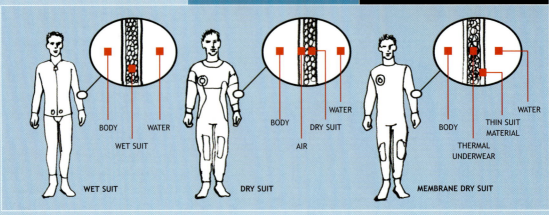

WET SUIT   DRY SUIT   MEMBRANE DRY SUIT

a low-pressure direct feed (similar to that on the BCD) to feed air through a valve into the suit. This valve is usually positioned on the chest where it will not interfere with any of the BCD fittings.

As the diver ascends this air expands, and just as with the BCD, it must be dumped or he or she will accelerate to the surface. Many suits have automatic dump valves at the cuff and you can raise the arm with the valve above your head to make it the highest point when required. The dump valve can also be positioned just below the shoulder.

Although the buoyancy of a dry suit can be altered, a BCD is still necessary to maintain buoyancy if the suit is torn or cut and is therefore no longer airtight, as well as for additional buoyancy at the surface, where an inflated BCD is more comfortable than the pressure on the neck seal produced by inflating the dry suit for positive buoyancy.

Divers may require larger fins to fit over dry suit bootees and many divers, particularly women, find it more comfortable to use small weights fixed around their ankles to help keep their legs down in the water.

Dry suit undergarments can be varied for the ambient temperature, from easily washed tracksuits through thicker synthetic pile 'woolly bears'

(polar fleece) to the warm but more difficult to launder fabric Thinsulate, which stays warm even if it gets wet.

Despite the term, dry suits are rarely completely dry, as both leaks and perspiration inevitably lead to damp undergarments.

Dry suit warning

Unlike wet suits there are several things that can go wrong when diving with a dry suit, from uncontrolled ascents to feet-first ascents where air migrates to and is trapped in the suit's legs.

All training agencies run courses on how to

avoid the pitfalls of dry suit diving and novices should take one of these before attempting to dive in a dry suit.

above left DRY SUITS ARE THE CHOICE OF DIVERS OPERATING IN EXTREMELY COLD CONDITIONS, SUCH AS DIVING UNDER ICE, AS THEY ALLOW DIVERS TO WEAR WARM UNDERGARMENTS.
above right STRETCHABLE NEOPRENE DRY SUITS FOLLOW THE CONTOURS OF THE DIVER'S BODY.

Scuba cylinders

Scuba cylinders are made of either steel or aluminium. Steel cylinders are more resistant to abrasion damage and have good buoyancy characteristics, but without proper care they may rust both inside and outside. Aluminium cylinders are more easily damaged by abrasion and require thicker walls to take the same internal pressure as steel cylinders. They are heavier but more positively buoyant than an equivalent capacity of a steel cylinder. Although aluminium corrodes in the same way as steel rusts, the thin coating of aluminium oxide formed actually inhibits further corrosion.

Scuba cylinder valves

Scuba cylinders are supplied fitted with on-off valves but divers may wish to convert single systems to a twin system with a connecting manifold — a common configuration for attaching a single regulator to a twin set. Some valves are universal, with a screw-type DIN socket and removable yoke connector (A-clamp) socket. The one valve is used both for filling the cylinder and for connection to the regulator.

Valves for steel scuba cylinders have taper threads and are fitted with plumber's PTFE sealing tape. Valves for aluminium cylinders have parallel threads and are sealed with an 'O'-ring. Within the cylinder the valve has a narrow pipe about 25mm (1in) long designed to prevent moisture or scale from restricting the airflow through the valve when the cylinder is inverted. Scuba cylinder valves may incorporate a 'burst disk' — a thin copper disk that bursts and vents off air under conditions of extreme heat or if the cylinder is overfilled. Cylinder valve to regulator 'O'-ring seals rely more on air pressure for a seal than the pressure created by tightening the yoke connector or DIN fittings. 'O'-rings deteriorate and will not seal if there are salt crystals or dirt on their surface. (Dive operators and dive boats are often short of these 'O'-rings so always carry your own spares.) Never use force to close the valve and when opening the valve to feed air to your regulator, turn it anticlockwise until it is fully open and then close it again by half a turn. This will prevent it from seizing in the open position.

above SCUBA CYLINDERS RANGE IN SIZE FROM 6-18 LITRES (49-148 CU FT) WATER CAPACITY AND COME IN VARIOUS LENGTHS TO SUIT EACH INDIVIDUAL DIVER'S HEIGHT. IN WARM WATER THEY ARE USUALLY USED SINGLY, THOUGH SMALL DIVERS MAY FIND A TWIN SET (MADE UP FROM TWO SMALLER CYLINDERS) MORE COMFORTABLE TO WEAR THAN A SINGLE LARGE CYLINDER. IN COLD WATER IT IS COMMON TO USE A TWIN SET MADE UP FROM TWO LARGER CYLINDERS.

right STEEL CYLINDERS (LEFT) HAVE TAPER THREADS SEALED WITH PLUMBER'S PTFE SEALING TAPE. ALUMINIUM CYLINDERS (RIGHT) HAVE PARALLEL THREADS AND ARE SEALED WITH AN 'O'-RING.

top COUNTRIES USING THE METRIC SYSTEM REFER TO CYLINDERS BY THEIR INTERNAL WATER CAPACITY IN LITRES AND THEIR WORKING PRESSURE IN BARS. COUNTRIES USING THE IMPERIAL SYSTEM REFER TO CYLINDERS BY THEIR AIR CAPACITY IN CUBIC FEET AT FULL WORKING PRESSURE. CYLINDERS HAVE THESE FIGURES STAMPED ON THE NECK, WHERE THE CYLINDER WALL IS AT ITS THICKEST, TOGETHER WITH ANY OTHER FIGURES AND TEST DATES REQUIRED BY LAW IN THE COUNTRY WHERE THE CYLINDERS ARE SOLD.

above AN ANNUAL INTERNAL INSPECTION OF CYLINDERS IS MANDATORY.

Care of scuba cylinders

For your own safety and that of whoever fills your scuba cylinders, they should be:

■ Handled carefully.
■ Regularly tested both visually and hydrostatically.
■ Never filled to more than their certified working pressure.
■ Rinsed outside with fresh water after use in salt water.
■ Filled with air slowly in a water bath to conduct away some of the heat produced.
■ Kept away from strong heat, including the sun.
■ Carefully secured for safe transportation.
■ Never breathed dry or otherwise emptied, except for visual inspection.

If a cylinder has been breathed dry underwater, it must be washed out with fresh water and allowed to dry thoroughly before being refilled, in case the ambient pressure has forced water into it.

If a cylinder has been in a fire, it should be thrown away.

Water can enter the cylinder in the following ways:

■ Poor compressor maintenance including overdue filter changes.
■ Breathing the cylinder dry underwater.
■ Leaving the valve open where there is condensation or high humidity.

Store cylinders upright with 10-20 bar (145-290 psi) of air pressure inside them. This reduces the concentration of oxygen and therefore any oxygen-related corrosion.

Aluminium cylinders have flat bases, but steel cylinders have round bases, so they cannot stand or be stored upright without being fitted with plastic or rubber 'cylinder boots'. Where boots are fitted to either type of cylinder they must drain the water easily and may be squared-off on the sides to stop the cylinders from rolling around when transported on their sides.

Regulators (Demand valves)

The regulator, also called a demand valve, is your most important piece of equipment, so it requires careful thinking about before you fork out hard-earned cash.

Basic regulators do not produce a large amount of air on demand, have few low-pressure ports and have a fixed single-size yoke-connector. On the plus side they are relatively simple, rarely malfunction and stand up to a lot of abuse, so they are popular with training schools as well as with divers who only dive occasionally in warm water. More expensive regulators will have low-pressure ports for inflating BCDs, dry suits or power tools and an additional second stage (octopus rig). They will easily supply the extra air required by these low-pressure ports and supply a large quantity of air on demand.

The standard unit is a single hose two stage regulator. The term single hose refers to the basic breathing unit; it does not include additional hoses that feed other devices. Two stage refers to the air pressure in the scuba cylinder being reduced in two stages to reach the pressure at which the diver breathes it.

The first stage of these regulators must reduce the cylinder pressure from around 200 bar (2900 psi) to a pressure within the hose that the second stage can handle, but still be high enough to overcome the ambient pressure on the lungs at depth. For most regulators this is approximately 10–13 bar (145–189 psi). First stages come in two basic types, piston or diaphragm.

Piston first stages are generally cheaper to manufacture and service and can be produced with a swivel arrangement for the part containing the low-pressure port outlets, but are hard to adjust in the field and water can enter the main casing resulting in corrosion.

Piston first stages can be balanced or unbalanced. In general, balanced first stages provide greater air flow, making it easier to breathe at depth, supply air to other items and enable two divers to simultaneously share the same air supply through both the main and alternate second stage. Unbalanced first stages become harder to breathe from as the cylinder pressure drops.

Diaphragm first stages do not allow water to enter the casing, reducing contamination and internal corrosion and leading to more consistent performance in cold water and

SECOND STAGE
ADJUSTMENT

STANDARD 300-BAR
DIN CONNECTOR

STANDARD YOKE-TO-DIN CONNECTOR

SWIVEL BASE WITH
EXTRA LOW-PRESSURE PORTS

top and middle A SINGLE HOSE, TWO STAGE REGULATOR IS THE STANDARD UNIT. ABOUT THIRTY PERCENT HAVE ADJUSTABLE SECOND STAGES. **bottom** THE LOW-PRESSURE PORTS ON THE REGULATOR ARE USED FOR INFLATING BCDS, DRY SUITS, POWER TOOLS AND AN EXTRA SECOND STAGE (OR OCTOPUS RIG).

between servicing. They are easy for qualified people to adjust in the field. For cold-water diving, some first stages can be environmentally sealed so that only a silicone- or alcohol-based fluid comes into contact with the piston or diaphragm and water cannot enter the system.

The illustration below depicts the most widely used type of basic second stage, which usually has the low-pressure hose passing over the diver's right shoulder. A purge button on the front opens the inlet valve and allows free-flowing air to clear any water out of the second stage before you fit it into your mouth. The exhaust valve is at the rear and directs exhaust bubbles to either side. This design has a definite top and bottom and has to be used the correct way up.

There is another type of second stage, where the diaphragm and exhaust valve are located at the side opposite from the low-pressure inlet hose. Smaller and lighter than the normal system, it can be used on either side of the face, so the low-pressure hose can pass over either shoulder and direct the exhaust bubbles clear of the face. This is particularly useful for photographers,

who can get closer to the camera eyepiece, and for use as an alternate air source, as a stressed diver cannot fit it into his or her mouth upside down by mistake.

When a diver inhales, the diaphragm is sucked inward and pushes against a demand lever that is connected to a one-way valve. This causes the valve to open and supplies the diver with air. Because the valve opens away from the airflow it is termed 'downstream'. This system is fail-safe; if the valve malfunctions it will remain open instead of closing and cutting off the air supply.

Alternate air source second stages, also known as octopus rigs, are connected to the regulator by their own low-pressure hose or to the direct feed for the BCD. Separate octopus rigs are usually yellow for easy identification by an out-of-air buddy. An octopus rig connected directly to the regulator can be easier to use if it has an extra long hose. Another alternate air source is a 'pony bottle', a 2–3 litre capacity (12–20 cu ft) cylinder with its own regulator that is strapped to the main cylinder.

Regulator maintenance

Ideally wash the regulator with fresh water while it is connected to the scuba cylinder valve with the air pressure still turned on. Otherwise, disconnect the regulator from the cylinder but leave it in position while turning the air in the cylinder slightly on, allowing gentle air flow to clear any moisture from the inlet of the first stage. Securely fit the dust cap and keep the first stage higher than the second stage while rinsing with fresh water. Do not press the purge button.

Regularly inspect the external filter of the first stage. A greenish colour shows that water has entered the first stage, and might be inside a recently used cylinder; a reddish filter indicates rust from a steel cylinder; and a blackish or oily filter indicates a cylinder filled from a defective compressor or compressor filter system. Have the regulator serviced after six months of heavy use or one year of light use, or at any time if there is a problem with its breathing output or any visible damage.

When a regulator is fitted to an air cylinder, point the pressure gauge away from other people when you turn on the air, as the glass may blow out. Check that the cylinder is full by reading the pressure gauge and listen for a leaking 'O'-ring. If the 'O'-ring is leaking, replace it.

INLET HOSE · INHALE · SPRING · MOUTHPIECE · EXHAUST VALVE CLOSED · AIR CHAMBER · VALVE OPENS LETTING AIR IN · PURGE BUTTON · WATER CHAMBER · DIAPHRAGM IS BOWED

EXHALE · EXHAUST VALVE OPEN · VALVE CLOSES · DIAPHRAGM IS STRAIGHT

MODERN SECOND STAGES USE LIGHTWEIGHT PLASTIC WHERE POSSIBLE TO REDUCE THEIR WEIGHT AND HAVE 'DOWNSTREAM' VALVES.

Instrumentation and accessories

Because of the effects of time and depth on scuba divers, there is certain information that is required on every dive. This includes:

- The maximum depth reached during the dive.
- The depth you are at any stage in the dive.
- The actual time spent underwater (bottom time).
- The current pressure in the air cylinder.

Divers must carry instruments that provide at least these facts, as well as a dive planner, decompression tables or a diving computer in case the planned bottom time or no-decompression time is exceeded, and a waterproof compass in case the visibility underwater deteriorates.

Submersible pressure gauges

The only way to tell how much air is left in a scuba cylinder is with a pressure gauge. These are connected to the high-pressure port of the first stage. Some divers fit a console to this gauge so that they can have most of their instruments together in one place.

The commonest mechanical pressure gauge is the oil-filled Bourdon type, a circular or spiral-shaped oil-filled tube sealed at one end and closed with a flexible diaphragm at the other.

When the high-pressure hose is connected to the outside of the diaphragm, the resulting pressure transmitted to the oil in the tube tends to straighten out the tube. The actual amount that the tube straightens is small so the far end of the tube connects, via a series of levers and gears that magnify the movement, to a pointer that moves across a pressure scale.

Depth gauges

Depth gauges inform the diver of the maximum depth reached. As the diver descends, a pointer moves up the scale while pushing another secondary pointer ahead of it. When the diver ascends the main pointer moves back down the scale but the secondary pointer remains where it is, giving the maximum depth reached. The secondary pointer has to be zeroed before each dive.

Underwater watches

Diving computers (refer to p72) have superseded underwater watches but batteries can fail, so unless you dive with two computers for backup, you should also dive with an underwater watch. Only watches quoted as suitable for depths of 200m (600ft) or more should be used for diving.

Digital diving watches should have a back light so that they can be read in dim light or at night and will include a stopwatch function, which should

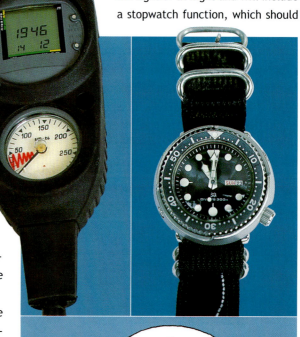

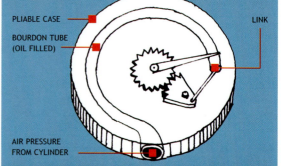

PLIABLE CASE

BOURDON TUBE (OIL FILLED)

LINK

AIR PRESSURE FROM CYLINDER

top left and above A SUBMERSIBLE PRESSURE GAUGE, SUCH AS THE OIL-FILLED BOURDON TUBE, IS USED TO READ CYLINDER PRESSURE.

top right ANALOGUE UNDERWATER WATCHES HAVE A ROTATING BEZEL THAT IS ALIGNED WITH THE MINUTE HAND AT THE START OF EACH DIVE.

be activated at the beginning of the dive to indicate elapsed time. Digital watches may have small activating buttons, which are difficult to operate with cold hands or when wearing gloves.

Analogue watches should have fluorescent hands and numerals for reading in dim light or at night, and a rotating ratcheted bezel. The bezel is aligned with the minute hand at the start of a dive so that when you next read it, the difference between this time and how far the minute hand has moved round the bezel, is the elapsed time.

Diving compass

Diving compasses are identical to land compasses except for being waterproof. Compasses are not required on most dives, but sudden changes in conditions or currents can seriously reduce visibility. For this reason it is wise to always have one permanently attached to your console or BCD so that it is there if you suddenly require it.

Knives

Diving knives are not for defence but are used for prying, digging, measuring, knocking against the main cylinder to attract another diver's attention and most importantly, for cutting ropes, baggage nets, fishing nets, fishing lines and seaweed, all of which could entangle divers and are particularly dangerous underwater.

Serrated blades are very effective for cutting ropes; normal knife blades are not efficient when cutting discarded monofilament fishing nets or lines because monofilament stretches. Some knives have a small sharp groove for cutting monofilament line but several tools have been specially designed for this use and many divers prefer cut-through-anything shears.

Underwater lights

Underwater lights (torches) come in all shapes, sizes and powers. Those used to illuminate divers and wrecks in daylight can be large and powerful but lights used on night dives should be of low power to avoid scaring shy marine creatures and sending them into hiding. Stronger lights are normally powered by rechargeable nickel-cadmium batteries whereas low-power lights can also be powered by alkaline batteries.

Spares

Last but not least, all divers should keep with their kit a waterproof box containing the tools and spare parts they are most likely to require when out diving. These include both flat and Phillips screwdrivers, spanners, Allen keys, extra mask and fin straps, scuba cylinder valve to regulator 'O'-rings, silicone grease, spare batteries for lights and diving computers, an additional mouthpiece and cable tie for the regulator's second stage and fish-hooks for removing old 'O'-rings.

top BY ATTACHING A CONSOLE TO THE PRESSURE GAUGE, THE DEPTH GAUGE AND COMPASS CAN BE CONVENIENTLY KEPT TOGETHER.
above A STURDY DIVE KNIFE IS ESSENTIAL FOR CUTTING ROPES OR FISHING NETS. ATTACH THE KNIFE TO THE OUTSIDE OF YOUR LOWER LEG, WHERE IT CAN BE EASILY GRASPED IF NEEDED.

Basic Training

no reputable diving establishment will supply you with full scuba cylinders or allow you to dive without an instructor unless you have a certification card ('C'-card) from a recognized training agency to prove that you are suitably trained.

There are two ways to receive diving training: enrol with a diving club for several months of weekly training sessions in a club environment; or take an intensive course with a specialized dive school.

Dive schools aim to make their students competent to dive in relatively easy conditions, such as in the warm tropical waters encountered while on holiday. Courses run by clubs take longer, but the training often includes specialist courses necessary to dive in colder water or more demanding situations.

Basic scuba equipment

New students must first become familiar with the basic scuba equipment and learn how to check it before use. Full scuba cylinders usually have a dust cap or strip of tape over their valve outlet to signify that they have been filled. Remove this and open the cylinder valve briefly to clear any water or dust from it. Check the valve's cylinder-to-regulator 'O'-ring and wipe a wet finger around it to remove salt crystals and help it to form a good seal. Slip the regulator first-stage connector over the valve's outlet, making sure it fits the recess machined into the cylinder valve, then tighten the yoke-connector ('A'-clamp) or DIN fitting.

Point the pressure gauge away from yourself and any other divers in case its glass blows out and open the valve slightly while listening for the sound of leaking air. If you can hear a leak you may not have fitted the regulator to the valve correctly, so close the valve and try fitting the regulator again. If you still hear a leak then either you require a new cylinder-to-regulator 'O'-ring or the fitting on the regulator is the wrong size. Once you have obtained the correct fitting, open the valve until you feel resistance, then close it by a quarter turn. Check the pressure gauge to make sure your cylinder is full.

Place the second stage mouthpiece in your mouth and get used to breathing through it. (You may have to try several before you find one that is comfortable.) While breathing through the second stage, view the pressure gauge; if the needle swings drastically, then something is wrong and the regulator should be serviced.

Once you have confirmed that you have a full cylinder, close the cylinder valve, remove the regulator first stage and fit the BCD. First close the valve and then release the air pressure by depressing the purge button at the centre of the front of the second stage. You will then be able to undo the regulator-to-cylinder valve yoke or DIN connector and remove the regulator.

Which training agency?

There is little difference in the quality of training provided by recognized training agencies such as the US-based Professional Association of Diving Instructors (PADI) and National Association of Underwater Instructors (NAUI), the British Sub-Aqua Club (BS-AC), or any of the many agencies affiliated to the World Underwater Federation (Confédération Mondiale des Activités Subaquatics — CMAS). (Refer to diving grades p11.)

Lectures will be given on the science, physiology and first aid that relate to diving, as well as dive planning. Some agencies also cover decompression in their basic training. Most agencies require a short swimming test, with and without snorkel equipment, to prove that you are comfortable and confident in the water.

right CLEARING YOUR MASK UNDERWATER, AND REPLACING IT IF IT IS ACCIDENTLY DISLODGED, ARE ESSENTIAL SKILLS WHICH ALL NEW DIVERS MUST MASTER. WITH PRACTICE THEY WILL SOON BECOME ROUTINE.

Filling the BCD emergency cylinder

If your BCD has a refillable emergency cylinder, you should fill it before fitting the regulator. Ensure that the main scuba cylinder is at full working pressure, remove the emergency cylinder from your BCD by undoing its yoke-connector and connect the yoke-connector to the cylinder valve in the same way as you would connect your regulator first stage. Fully open the valve of the emergency cylinder and then slowly open the valve of the scuba cylinder to allow air to flow into the emergency cylinder. When the sound of air flowing between the two cylinders ceases, close both valves. The valve on the emergency cylinder has a purge button on a spring. You must depress this button to purge the air remaining between the valves before you can disconnect the emergency cylinder. Refit the emergency cylinder to the BCD and briefly open the valve to make sure that the BCD inflates correctly.

1 INSPECT THE CYLINDER-TO-REGULATOR 'O'-RING FOR CUTS, HAIRS AND SALT AND WIPE IT WITH A WET FINGER TO CLEAN IT.

2 TURN THE VALVE ON MOMENTARILY TO CLEAN AWAY ANY DUST.

3 FIT THE REGULATOR FIRST-STAGE YOKE-CONNECTOR (A-CLAMP OR DIN FITTING) TO THE CYLINDER AND DO IT UP.

FIT THE BCD EMERGENCY CYLINDER TO THE SCUBA CYLINDER AND FILL IT UP SLOWLY BY OPENING BOTH VALVES, THEN CLOSE BOTH VALVES AND DEPRESS THE PURGE BUTTON ON THE EMERGENCY CYLINDER TO ENABLE THE TWO CYLINDERS TO BE DISCONNECTED.

Fitting the BCD and regulator to the cylinder

BCDs have one or more straps (called cam-bands) that fit around the scuba cylinder, with the BCD backpack facing the outlet of the cylinder valve and far enough down the scuba cylinder that the cylinder valve is just higher than the top of the BCD backpack. Do not undo these straps completely to fit them around the cylinder, as they are threaded through a buckle in such a way that they will not be able to come loose by mistake. Once in position, pull the straps tight and then force the cam (lever) over on itself until it locks into position.

Now refit the regulator first stage so that the low-pressure hose for the primary second stage (the one you intend to breathe through, not an octopus rig) passes over the necessary shoulder for the second stage to be the correct way up. Connect up any low-pressure direct feed hose to the BCD, fit all hoses into their retaining clips or Velcro tabs and turn the cylinder on. Now, with the help of a buddy to hold the weight of the equipment, slip into the shoulder straps of the BCD. Make sure that nothing is trapped beneath them and adjust the straps for comfort, then lean forward and tighten the waist strap. Bend backward and check that the regulator first-stage does not hit your head; if it does, it is too high. You can lower the height of the regulator first stage by loosening the shoulder straps of the BCD — but if they are too loose, the regulator first stage can hit your head if you jump into the water, and you will need to lower the scuba cylinder within the cam-band of the BCD.

At this stage, fit the primary second stage into your mouth and try breathing through it. If the hose to the primary second stage is too short or too long, it can be altered by turning the cylinder slightly to the left or right within the cam-band of the BCD, until the mouthpiece fits comfortably.

Pool training

You are now ready to try breathing underwater. Place the primary second stage mouthpiece in your mouth, fit your mask and climb into the shallow end of the swimming pool (there is no need to wear fins). With the instructor standing by, hold onto the side of the pool and submerge your head by bending face-down into the water. This

THE FIRST STEP IN DIVE TRAINING IS LEARNING TO BREATHE UNDER-WATER USING SCUBA EQUIPMENT. IT SEEMS UNNATURAL INITIALLY, BUT YOU WILL SOON LEARN TO RELAX AND BREATHE NORMALLY.

does not feel natural. At first there will be a tendency to hold your breath and you will be conscious of each breath sounding surprisingly loud, but you will slowly relax.

Next you must learn to become correctly weighted. Wear all the equipment you expect to use in the pool (wet suit, fins, mask, BCD, etc.) and be sure that you understand how to release the weight belt quickly if you have a problem. Begin by fitting one small lead weight to the weight belt, put it on and do it up. Now bend forward in the water and let your legs float up behind you. One weight is unlikely to be enough so you will have to keep adding more weights until your body slowly sinks to the bottom. You have now found the correct weight to wear in fresh water when dressed as you are. (You will require more weight in salt water or if wearing a thicker wet suit.) Practise how to release the weight belt with one hand in an emergency.

Clearing the second stage mouthpiece

Before you venture into deeper water you should learn how to clear the mask and second stage mouthpiece of water. Practise by kneeling on the bottom of the shallow end of the pool so that you can stand with your head clear of the water if you encounter any problems.

When properly fitted in your mouth, the regulator second stage will not allow water to leak in unless the exhaust valve is damaged or has collected some sand or grit that prevents it from forming a seal. However, if the mouthpiece is removed from the diver's mouth for any reason, the second stage downstream of its valve will fill with water. If this occurs, it is easily cleared of water by breathing out through the regulator before you breathe in. If your second stage has a definite top and bottom, you must ensure that you fit it into your mouth correctly, with the exhaust valve at the bottom. If you have insufficient breath left to clear the second stage, you can clear it by holding it away from your mouth and depressing the purge button.

TO CLEAR THE SECOND STAGE OF WATER, HOLD THE MOUTHPIECE ABOVE YOUR HEAD AND PRESS THE PURGE BUTTON.

The mouthpiece itself must always remain at the lowest point of the second stage to ensure that the air inside the second stage keeps the water out. To do this, hold the second stage above your head with the mouthpiece pointing downward. Then press the purge button and tilt your head back, so that you can refit the mouthpiece into your mouth while it continues to be the lowest point of the second stage. Once the mouthpiece is back in your mouth, you should breathe out before you breathe in.

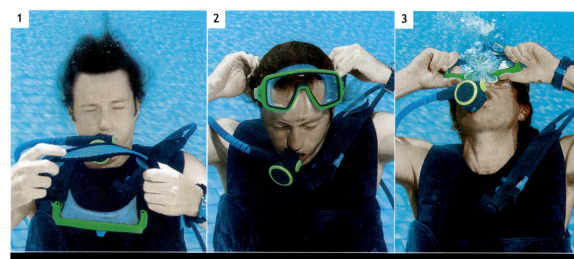

1 TO FIT THE MASK, HOLD THE STRAP AWAY FROM THE MASK AND ENSURE THE MASK IS THE CORRECT WAY UP.

2 FIT THE STRAP BEHIND THE HEAD AND PLACE THE MASK OVER YOUR FACE, MAKING SURE THAT NO HAIR IS TRAPPED.

3 TILT THE HEAD BACK, PRESS THE TOP EDGE OF THE MASK AND SNORT OUT THROUGH THE NOSE TO FORCE WATER OUT OF THE MASK.

Clearing the mask

All masks will leak at some time and other divers can easily knock them off your face. If the mask is fitted with a purge valve, you can clear most of the water by snorting out through your nose into the mask. However purge valves cannot be relied on, and often collect grit, becoming the cause of the leak. It is more effective to tilt the head back, press one hand against the top of the mask and snort out strongly through the nose to displace the water through the bottom of the mask.

To practise for a situation where your mask is knocked off, remove it completely. Make sure that it is the correct way up, hold the strap in one hand and the mask in the other. If necessary, clear any hair from the forehead, fit the mask over your face, pull the strap over the back of your head, tilt your head back, press the top edge of the mask and snort into it to clear out any water. This should be practised in progressively deeper water.

Sharing air

Before you leave the safety of shallow water you must practise sharing air in case you or your buddy run out of air. If you keep a constant check on your pressure gauge and begin your ascent when the cylinder is about one-quarter full, you should never run low on air underwater. However you can have an unforeseen problem, such as a burst 'O'-ring between the cylinder valve and regulator first stage, a sudden leak in the high-pressure hose or having to swim against a strong current, and may need to rely on another source.

The easiest way to share air is via an alternate air supply, or octopus rig, attached to the BCD direct feed, as then you both have your own second stage.

To share air, or buddy-breathe, signal to your buddy that you are out of air, then take their alternate air supply, make sure that it is the correct way up and that the mouthpiece remains pointing downward. Purge the unit of water, place it into your mouth and breathe out before you breathe in. When sharing air, buddies should hold onto each other's BCD shoulder straps and slowly ascend.

As there is always the possibility that one of you does not have an alternate air supply, you must train for this situation, first on land and then in shallow water. Signal to your buddy that you are out of air, approach him or her face to face and each take a firm hold of the other's BCD shoulder straps. The diver who still has air (the donor) should take two breaths, then pass his or her second stage so that it is close to the recipient's mouth with the mouthpiece pointing downward. The recipient should take the second stage, keep the mouthpiece pointing downward, purge it, fit it into his or her mouth, breathe out and then take two breaths before handing it back to the donor. Repeat this cycle until both surface.

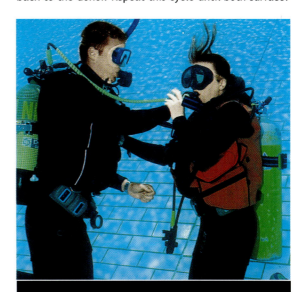

BUDDY-BREATHING, WHERE TWO DIVERS SHARE A SINGLE AIR SUPPLY, IS MADE EASIER BY USING AN ALTERNATE AIR SUPPLY (OCTOPUS RIG), BUT DIVERS MUST ALSO BE PREPARED TO SHARE ONE AIR SUPPLY.

This exercise is intended to be practised for an emergency situation where both divers would be slowly ascending, so whenever either diver is not actually breathing through the mouthpiece, he should exhale gently. Once divers are comfortable with this exercise they can repeat it while swimming horizontally.

In a real life situation, the diver who is out of air is likely to be stressed and may not behave rationally. If you do not have a highly visible octopus rig, he or she may grab for the second stage that is actually in your mouth. It is wise to be prepared for this, so always have your own alternate air supply and be prepared to use it yourself if your buddy grabs your primary second stage.

Hand signals

IDEALLY THE HAND SIGNALS used to communicate underwater should be standardized among all dive training agencies, so that every diver would be able to recognize another diver's signals; but unfortunately this is not so and discrepancies frequently occur.

If you dive with someone who has been trained with a different agency, you should always compare hand signals before you dive. In situations of stress, divers are likely to revert to the hand signals they have been trained with so you need to be able to recognize your instructor's or buddy's hand signals.

OK?/OK

OK?/OK

NOT OK

COME HERE

STOP/HOLD IT/STAY THERE

GO DOWN/GOING DOWN

WHICH DIRECTION?

GO THAT WAY

YOU LEAD, I'LL FOLLOW

ME/WATCH ME

ME/WATCH ME (ALT. VERSION)

TAKE IT EASY/SLOW DOWN

LOW ON AIR

GET WITH YOUR BUDDY

HOLD HANDS

OUT OF AIR

BUDDY-BREATHE/SHARE AIR

BUDDY-BREATHE/SHARE AIR (ALT. VERSION)

EARS NOT CLEARING

GO UP/GOING UP

DISTRESS/HELP

Training in deeper water

You are now ready to venture into deeper water. Swim to the deep end of the pool, signal to your instructor that you are about to descend and expel any excess air from your BCD. There are two methods of descending from the surface: feet first or head first. With either method it is important to be correctly weighted. If you have too much weight, you will have a rapid and possibly unsafe descent, could well experience problems with your ears, sinuses and mask squeeze, and could possibly crash into live coral and kill it. If you have too little weight you may have to make several tiring attempts to get below the surface.

If you suffer from equalization problems or are carrying anything, it is easiest to descend in an upright position (feet first), and if you are correctly weighted, breathing out hard will be enough to initiate your descent. If you do not suffer equalization problems, you can descend head first by making a surface dive, often referred to as a duck-dive.

Descents should be slow and controlled and you should keep an eye on your buddies so that you stay together but do not collide underwater. Ascents should be slower than your smallest bubbles. Get into the habit of breathing out as you ascend and checking above you to ensure that you are not likely to bump into anything or anyone on the surface. Once on the surface, look around you, inflate your BCD if necessary, and give the OK signal to your instructor.

Mobility and buoyancy

To be comfortably mobile underwater you should be neutrally buoyant (able to maintain your position in the water). If you are too buoyant you will have difficulty in keeping down to the same level, while if you are not buoyant enough you will tend to sink. You require sufficient weight to leave the surface without floundering but not too much or you will sink too quickly. (Remember that underwater lights and cameras also act as weights and affect your overall buoyancy.)

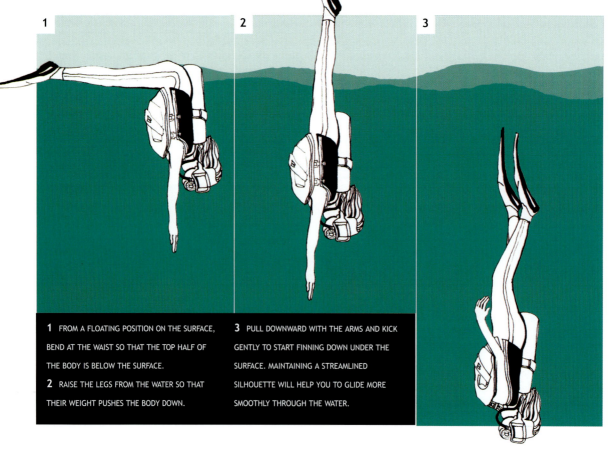

1 FROM A FLOATING POSITION ON THE SURFACE, BEND AT THE WAIST SO THAT THE TOP HALF OF THE BODY IS BELOW THE SURFACE.

2 RAISE THE LEGS FROM THE WATER SO THAT THEIR WEIGHT PUSHES THE BODY DOWN.

3 PULL DOWNWARD WITH THE ARMS AND KICK GENTLY TO START FINNING DOWN UNDER THE SURFACE. MAINTAINING A STREAMLINED SILHOUETTE WILL HELP YOU TO GLIDE MORE SMOOTHLY THROUGH THE WATER.

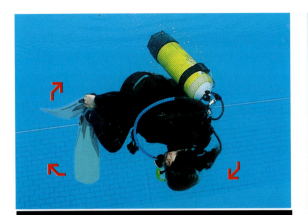

FORWARD ROLL – BEGIN FROM A STANDING POSITION, TAKE A DEEP BREATH IN TO INCREASE YOUR BUOYANCY AND AS YOUR BODY RISES, PERFORM A FORWARD ROLL, PULLING THE WATER TOWARD YOU WITH YOUR HANDS AND ARMS TO DRAW YOUR BODY AROUND. WHEN BACK IN A STANDING POSITION, BREATHE OUT TO REDUCE YOUR BUOYANCY.

MAINTAINING BUOYANCY – BY REGULATING YOUR BREATHING YOU CAN CONTROL YOUR BUOYANCY. WHEN YOU ARE NEUTRALLY BUOYANT, YOU WILL BE ABLE TO MAINTAIN YOUR POSITION AT THE DESIRED DEPTH.

You are most buoyant near the surface. When you descend, you lose buoyancy as your equipment compresses. A small loss in buoyancy can be corrected for by how deeply you breathe. Taking large breaths causes your chest to expand and you will become more buoyant. Forcibly breathing out or shallow breathing causes your chest to contract and you will become less buoyant.

As you dive deeper you must feed air into your BCD to compensate for your loss of buoyancy. As you ascend you need to dump (vent off) air from your BCD to compensate for the increasing buoyancy. Similarly, as your underwater time increases you will need to dump air from your BCD to compensate for the increasing buoyancy of the scuba cylinder as its air supply is used up.

To feed air into your BCD, either press a button on the direct feed from your regulator or, if you have one, briefly open the valve on the small emergency cylinder.

To orally fill the BCD when underwater, unclip the corrugated tube, breathe in from your regulator, remove the second stage mouthpiece from your mouth, replace it with the mouthpiece attached to the corrugated tube and press the BCD purge button before exhaling into the corrugated tube. You may have to do this several times, so release the BCD purge button before taking your mouth from the BCD to breathe from your regulator, or

TO ORALLY INFLATE THE BCD, INHALE FROM YOUR REGULATOR, THEN EXHALE INTO THE MOUTHPIECE ATTACHED TO THE BCD ORAL INFLATION TUBE, REPEATING THE EXERCISE UNTIL THE BCD IS INFLATED.

air will escape from the BCD and water will flow in. You must also clear the regulator's second stage mouthpiece before you return it to your mouth.

There are various familiarization exercises that help overcome feelings of disorientation and improve your confidence underwater as you learn automatically to control small changes in buoyancy through breathing.

To maintain neutral buoyancy, position yourself clear of the bottom and try to relax. Observe how taking deep breaths causes you to rise, while breathing out deeply makes you sink. Regulate your breathing until you learn to maintain your body at a constant depth.

Ditch and retrieve

When learning how to remove and replace the BCD, scuba cylinder and regulator, start by kneeling on the bottom of the pool. Keep the regulator's primary second stage in your mouth and take off the BCD. Place the BCD and cylinder on the bottom of the pool. You will not have any trouble with buoyancy so long as you keep your weight belt on. Take a medium breath, turn

last, but hold onto it while you take a deep breath. Turn off the air, remove the primary second stage from your mouth and lay it on the cylinder, then carefully let go of the weight belt and swim to the surface.

While treading water, look down and locate the weight belt. This must be your first target, as without it you will be too buoyant. Take a medium breath, dive down to the weight belt and lay it over one knee.

the air off, remove the regulator primary second stage from your mouth, place it on the scuba cylinder and give an OK signal to your instructor. Now reverse the process. Turn the air on, keep the mouthpiece pointing downward and purge it of water. Tilt your head back,

DITCHING A BCD AND CYLINDER

1 LOOSEN THE BCD SHOULDER STRAPS

2 and **3** REMOVE THE ARMS IN TURN FROM THE BCD SHOULDER STRAPS, UNDO THE BCD WAIST BELT AND TAKE OFF THE BCD.

4 LAY THE BCD AND CYLINDER IN FRONT OF YOU ON THE BOTTOM OF THE POOL

place the mouthpiece into your mouth, then breathe out before breathing in. Now put your arms through the BCD shoulder straps and lift the BCD and cylinder over your head so that it slips on. Do up the waist strap, making sure that it does not interfere with the quick release buckle of your weight belt, and then give your instructor another OK sign.

Once you are confident with removing and replacing the BCD in shallow water, you can try a full 'ditch and retrieve' procedure. While the instructor watches from the bottom, take off your BCD, scuba cylinder, mask and regulator first stage. Take your weight belt off

Next locate the cylinder valve. Turn on the air, holding the regulator's second stage so that its mouthpiece is pointing downward. Purge it of water before fitting it into your mouth and breathe out before you breathe in. Now that you have established your air supply and are correctly weighted, you can take your time locating your mask. Clear the mask of water, refit it, then put the BCD back on and give an OK signal to your instructor.

The Buddy System

FOR SAFETY, DIVERS USE THE buddy system — that is, they dive in pairs. Buddies double-check each other's equipment and keep a constant watch on one another, so that they will notice quickly if one of them requires assistance. Before they enter the water a buddy pair should check the following:

■ That each diver understands the hand signals to be used.

■ That each other's air supply is fully turned on.

■ Check the pressure gauge to ensure the cylinder is full.

■ That the BCD harness and weights system are not fouling any other equipment. If one buddy has an integrated weight system, check that you both know how to release it.

■ That the direct feeds are fitted correctly to the BCD and, if worn, the dry suit.

■ That you each know how to inflate or deflate your buddy's BCD and, if worn, dry suit.

■ That each buddy has either a diving computer or a watch, depth gauge and dive planner or decompression tables.

■ That each diver has a correctly fitted mask, fins, snorkel, knife and compass.

■ That there are no dangling straps or trapped hoses.

■ That you each understand the action to be taken in the event of separation.

Once in the water you should check each other's equipment for damage, give each other and any boat cover the OK signal, each give the descent signal and make sure that the other is ready by giving the OK signal, then descend together.

■ Keep close together. If one buddy has problems with equalizing ears or sinuses, stop and wait until both of you are able to continue descending.

■ If one diver is deploying a surface marker buoy, the other should be on the opposite side to avoid becoming entangled.

■ If one diver wishes to change direction, this should be conveyed to the other and an agreement on the new direction must be acknowledged.

■ When the dive is over, or one of you has reached a pre-arranged air pressure on your gauge, give each other the ascent signal and keep together while slowly ascending.

■ In poor visibility, tie a line (buddy line) between you as an aid to keeping together.

■ If buddies become separated they should first search for each other. If not successful within one minute, each buddy should abandon the dive, ascend slowly and reunite on the surface.

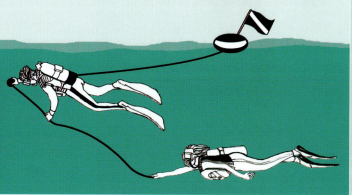

top right BUDDIES SHOULD CHECK EACH OTHER'S EQUIPMENT BEFORE DIVING.

right WHEN USING A SURFACE MARKER BUOY AND/OR BUDDY LINE, FOR SAFETY REASONS, THESE SHOULD BE HELD IN THE HANDS, NOT TIED TO ANY EQUIPMENT.

Preparing for open water diving

In open water you will be venturing into an environment where there are hazards on the surface such as boats, other surface craft (e.g. jet-skis and windsurfers), and choppy water. Divers should learn the following procedures for safe ascent:

■ Give your buddy the 'ascend' signal and make sure that he or she understands by returning it.

■ Look up and fin gently towards the surface.

■ Watch each other so that you can keep together.

■ Ascend slower than your smallest bubbles and make sure that you breathe out.

■ Rotate your body to get an all-round view.

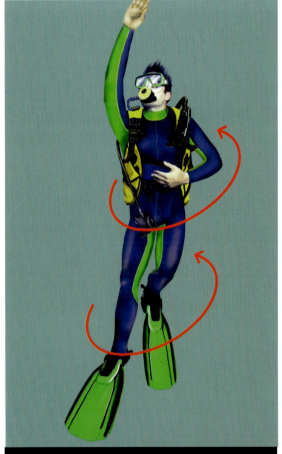

WHEN ASCENDING, ROTATE YOUR BODY TO CHECK IT IS CLEAR IN ALL DIRECTIONS. RAISE ONE ARM ABOVE YOUR HEAD AS YOU NEAR THE SURFACE FOR PROTECTION FROM BOATS AND OTHER SURFACE CRAFT.

■ Vent your BCD as necessary, while you ascend.

■ Hold one arm above your head as protection from unseen surface craft.

■ Once on the surface, check in all directions for approaching boats or surface craft.

■ Inflate your BCD on reaching the surface.

■ Give the OK signal to your buddy and also to any boat or shore cover.

■ Swim to the shore or boat (or wait for the boat to pick you up if you are on a drift dive).

If you have been out of air, the small amount of air left in your cylinder may have expanded enough to give you a few breaths when near to the surface, but it is unlikely to give enough air to inflate the BCD.

Some BCDs have a one-off-use carbon dioxide (CO_2) cylinder for surface inflation while others have an emergency cylinder fitted to the BCD that is filled from the scuba cylinder before each dive. You can also inflate BCDs orally (refer to p57).

So far you have trained in the pool under ideal conditions and possibly without an exposure suit. Lycra skin suits make little difference to your buoyancy, but all other exposure suits do, so you will have to sort out your buoyancy again when you get into the sea.

As well as the theory and practicalities of diving, you should have been taught basic first aid (refer to pp77/78), and how to give EAR (p78) and CPR (pp79/80).

For your first open water dive the instructor will give you a 'dive plan'. This is a briefing on what to expect during the dive, how deep you can go and for how long, any tests that are to be carried out and backup plans to use if things do not go quite the way envisaged.

You do your buddy checks, enter the water and do them again. If everything is fine, you both exchange OK signals and descend to the intended depth and complete any planned tests. If there is a current, you begin by swimming into it so that it will bring you back to your starting point when you return.

When the dive is over you will return to shore, disassemble and wash your equipment in fresh water, then have a debriefing. Do not be afraid to question anything you are not sure about. Congratulations! You have made your first open water dive.

Underwater navigation

Divers often utilize natural features such as rock or coral outcrops, gorgonian sea fans which grow at right angles to the prevailing current, or sand ripples which normally run parallel to the shoreline, but when the bottom is featureless, a compass is essential.

The centre line of a compass indicates the proposed direction of travel and the diver must keep his or her body in line with it. The magnetic needle can be affected by steel cylinders, dive knives, watches, electronic instruments, etc., so keep your compass clear of these items when taking a reading. Either mount the compass in a console or use both hands to hold it separately as far in front of, and in line with, the body as possible.

Compass points

Compasses have a centre line (called a lubber line) which marks the fore and aft ends of the compass; a needle or card that indicates magnetic north; and a rotating bezel or index marks that can be turned to line up with the north-pointing needle.

The compass itself is divided into 360° (degrees) which follow in a clockwise direction from 0° at north, through 90° at east, 180° at south, 270° at west and then back to north again at 360° or 0°.

An important part of diving is being able to find your way back to your starting point. As a last resort you can surface and swim back to your point of entry or, if boat diving, try to catch the attention of the boat crew and have the boat come to you, but there are several problems with this approach. If the swell or waves are high, then it will be difficult for the boat crew to see you. Even in calm water, swimming on the surface is more strenuous than swimming underwater as progress may be hindered by surface currents or wind. It is tempting to surface, take a sighting and compass bearing on your intended target and then descend to swim towards it. However it is not a good idea to do this more than once, as 'bounce' diving can lead to DCS. As far as decompression tables or a diving computer are concerned, this is the equivalent of surfacing and beginning another dive without taking a surface interval. If this happens, some diving computers will cease giving information until they consider that a suitable surface interval has passed.

There are three ways to practise using a compass. To estimate how far you travel along a particular bearing, simply count fin strokes and record the figures on an underwater slate. Begin with a simple out-and-back route, pick a time when there is no current and swim out along a bearing, maintaining a straight course and noting distinctive features on the seabed. When you have gone far enough, turn around through 180°, add 180° to the bearing you followed on the route out. You now have a reciprocal bearing to follow on the way back, noting the same features as on the way out.

Triangular dive patterns involve two turns. Set out along a compass bearing for a fixed time or number of fin strokes, then turn right through 120°, add 120° to the first compass bearing and follow the new bearing for the same time or number of fin strokes. Turn right again through 120°, add another 120° and follow the new bearing back to the starting point. Rectangular patterns involve three right-angle (90°) turns and you should travel along parallel sides of the rectangle for the same time or number of fin strokes.

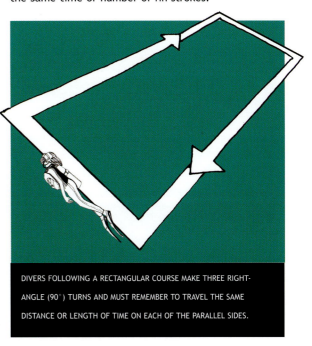

DIVERS FOLLOWING A RECTANGULAR COURSE MAKE THREE RIGHT-ANGLE (90°) TURNS AND MUST REMEMBER TO TRAVEL THE SAME DISTANCE OR LENGTH OF TIME ON EACH OF THE PARALLEL SIDES.

Sea Training & Dive Planning

In the excitement of making a first sea (open water) dive, novice divers should not overlook the importance of learning about the sea, as a sound knowledge of it will contribute greatly towards making scuba diving a safe and pleasurable experience.

Tides and currents

By understanding tides, divers can pick the best time to dive; neap tides and slack water for easy dives or photography, while spring tides and full flow offer more opportunities for encounters with pelagic fish species.

Tides are caused by the combined effect of the earth's spin and the gravitational attraction between the moon and the earth and, to a lesser extent, the sun and the earth. One tide cycle (from high to low water and back to high water again) usually takes 12 hours.

Spring tides, those of maximum range and strength, occur twice a month at the new and full moons. Stronger equinoctial spring tides occur at the new and full moons closest to the equinoxes, in March and September. Neap tides, those of minimum range and strength, occur twice a month at or near the first and last quarters of the moon. Ebb tides, which flow off a reef or land, can contain sediment that diminishes visibility underwater. Flood tides are those that flow onto a reef or land. If tides flow over a hard substrate the visibility will be good. When the tide is in full flow the current will be strong, especially if the water has travelled over a large expanse of open ocean without striking any land or shallow reefs to slow it down.

During the period on either side of low or high tide, when the tides are reversing direction, there will be a short period of slack water (when the current is either light or nonexistent). Local tide tables enable you to calculate flood and ebb tides and fast or slack water.

Differences in water temperature, wind blowing close to the surface of the sea, or the sun's heat on a shallow reef can all create currents, which may sometimes be nonexistent in the morning but get progressively stronger until mid-afternoon.

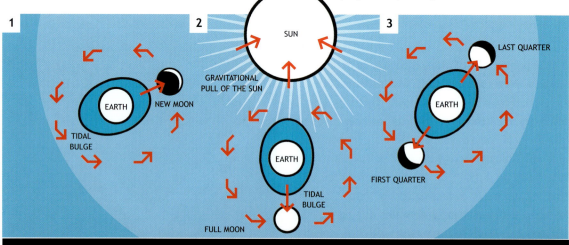

1 NEW MOON WITH THE SUN AND MOON ALIGNED, THEIR COMBINED GRAVITATIONAL PULL CREATES THE HIGHEST SPRING TIDES (MAXIMUM DIFFERENCE BETWEEN HIGH AND LOW WATER).

2 FULL MOON ALTHOUGH THE SUN AND THE MOON ARE IN LINE, THEIR GRAVITATIONAL PULL IS IN OPPOSITION; BUT THIS ALSO RESULTS IN SPRING TIDES.

3 FIRST AND LAST QUARTERS OF THE MOON THE SUN AND THE MOON ARE NOT ALIGNED; THIS PRODUCES NEAP TIDES, THOSE WITH LEAST VARIATION BETWEEN HIGH AND LOW TIDES.

Getting into the water

Diving from a beach

There are two ways of entering the water from a beach; either fit your fins to your feet and shuffle backwards into the water until it is deep enough to turn around and swim, or walk into the water while carrying your fins until the water is deep enough for swimming, and then use your buddy for support while you fit them. If there is surf it will be easier to fit your fins first and walk backwards into the water. Exiting the water is the reverse of entry.

Diving from rocks

Climbing over slippery or awkward rocks in full diving equipment can be difficult and you must have knowledge of the local tides. Low water could produce a large drop into the water, and the rocks may be too high for divers to be able to exit the water after the dive.

Wear hard-soled bootees and make several journeys to the water's edge, each time carrying as little equipment as possible. Leave one hand free to steady yourself on each trip. Choose a solid rock for support while putting on your fins and then sit at the water's edge

WHEN ENTERING THROUGH SURF, DIVERS OFTEN FIND IT EASIEST TO FIT THEIR FINS FIRST AND THEN WALK BACKWARDS INTO THE WATER.

and use your hands to lower yourself into the water. Only leap in if the water is clear and obviously deep. Time your entry so that you hit the water at the top of a swell or wave, then fin out hard to allow the backwash to carry you away from the rocks.

Time your exit so that you use the highest point of a wave or swell to lift you onto the rocks. If you fail, wait for the next wave. Avoid using channels or gullies for entry or exit, as these will have a stronger surge.

SIT ON THE ROCKS AND FIT YOUR MASK AND FINS BEFORE USING YOUR HANDS TO LOWER YOURSELF INTO THE WATER.

Entry from a jetty

THERE ARE TWO WAYS TO enter the water from a jetty, a long stride or a forward roll.

For the long stride entry (below), you should first inflate the BCD slightly, ensure your buddy is also ready and that the water is clear of other divers or obstructions. Hold the mask and regulator's primary second stage in place with one hand and use your other hand to push down the BCD waist strap so the scuba cylinder cannot bounce up and strike your neck when you enter the water. Take a long stride outward so the scuba cylinder is clear of the jetty. Swim clear of the entry point to allow other divers to enter the water.

For heights up to 1m (3ft) you can use a forward roll entry.

As you do not have to hold onto your diving gear your hands are free to carry other items. However cameras should be lowered into the water, or handed down to the diver by someone else.

Exiting the water onto a jetty will always be up steps or a ladder and ideally the water should be calm enough to enable you to remove your fins first.

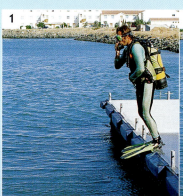

1 HOLD THE MASK AND PRIMARY SECOND STAGE REGULATOR WITH ONE HAND AND PUSH DOWN ON THE BCD STRAP WITH THE OTHER.

2 TAKE A LONG STRIDE OUT FROM THE JETTY, MAKING SURE YOUR CYLINDER IS CLEAR AND WILL NOT CATCH ON THE EDGE OF THE JETTY.

3 KEEP YOUR HANDS IN POSITION UNTIL YOU FLOAT BACK TO THE SURFACE, THEN LOCATE YOUR BUDDY AND MOVE CLEAR OF THE AREA.

1 A FORWARD ROLL ENTRY IS SUITABLE FOR HEIGHTS OF UP TO 1M (3FT).

2 FOLD YOUR BODY FORWARD SO THAT YOUR BACK HITS THE WATER FIRST.

3 KEEP YOUR HEAD AND LEGS TUCKED IN AS YOU ENTER THE WATER.

Boat diving

The most important thing with boat diving is for the person in charge (the skipper or divemaster) to have some way of monitoring that all divers are accounted for before the boat can move anywhere.

Entry from an inflatable or small boat

In small boats there is rarely enough room to move around, and it is usual to put on all equipment except fins and mask before boarding. The safest place to keep your mask is to hang it around your neck. Once on the boat, make room for other divers to board, sit on either of the boat's gunwale (side) seats or on an inflatable's side pontoon and put on your fins.

When you reach the dive site it is preferable for pairs of divers on opposite sides of the boat to enter the water at the same time, otherwise the boat will rock excessively. Usually the coxswain (helmsman) will check that the water behind each diving pair is clear and then give the order for them to enter the water.

Before entering the water, put your fins on, then fit your mask and put the regulator primary second stage into your mouth. Ensure your scuba cylinder is turned on, that the water behind you is clear and that your fins will not catch on anything on the floor of the boat. Hold your mask and regulator primary second stage in place with one hand and when the coxswain gives the order, roll over backward with your legs together. Once in the water, join your buddy and swim clear of the boat to give other divers clear water for entry.

To exit the water, hold onto the side of the boat, or the lifelines on the side of an inflatable, with one hand and with the other hand carefully release your weight belt and pass it into the boat. If your weights are integrated with your BCD, leave them attached. Next, undo your BCD waist strap, slacken or disconnect one

SMALL BOATS OR INFLATABLES ARE USUALLY CROWDED, SO DIVERS SHOULD KIT UP BEFORE BOARDING. ONE DIVER FROM EACH SIDE SHOULD ENTER THE WATER TOGETHER TO PREVENT CAPSIZING OR ROCKING.

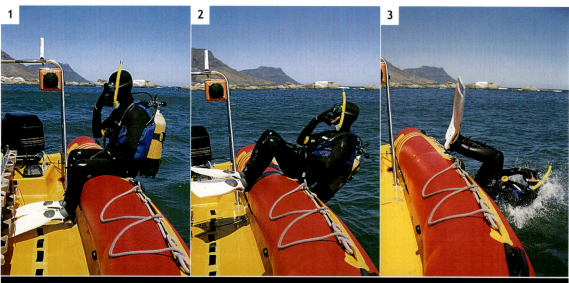

1 HOLD YOUR MASK AND REGULATOR PRIMARY SECOND STAGE IN PLACE AND PUSH DOWN ON YOUR BCD WAIST STRAP.

2 MAKE SURE YOUR FINS WILL NOT CATCH ONTO ANYTHING ON THE BOTTOM OF THE BOAT, THEN ROLL BACKWARD INTO THE WATER.

3 KEEP HOLDING ONTO YOUR MASK, REGULATOR AND BCD UNTIL YOU FLOAT BACK TO THE SURFACE.

of your BCD shoulder straps, take your second stage mouthpiece out of your mouth and slip your free arm out of the BCD. The BCD, regulator and scuba cylinder can then be lifted into the boat by someone who is already on board or clipped to lines (ropes) attached to the boat for retrieval once you are on board. At this stage, keep your fins and mask on.

With both hands, clasp the boat's gunwale, or the lifelines on an inflatable, then pull up with your arms and simultaneously kick with your fins. This will propel you far enough over the top of the gunwale or pontoon to get your body into the boat.

Once on board, take off your mask and fins, collect and tidy up your equipment and move to one side or to the end of the boat or inflatable to leave room for other divers to board.

At this stage, with all the gear that will be in the bottom of the boat, it is advisable to keep your mask around your neck to minimize the chance of breakage.

right IF YOUR WEIGHT BELT IS SEPARATE, TAKE IT OFF AND HAND IT INTO THE BOAT FIRST, BEING CAREFUL NOT TO DROP IT INTO THE WATER.

Surface navigation

When shore diving, locating a dive site is usually quite simple because the site generally has a direct relation to the entry point. However, fixing or finding an off-shore dive site is not as easy.

Nowadays Global Positioning Systems (GPS) are becoming relatively cheap, but if the dive site is within sight of the shore, most divers still rely on transits (marks). To do this, take a number of compass bearings that line up two or more lines of sight, where each line of sight itself lines up easily visible and fixed features, such as a lighthouse, tall building or natural feature.

Where these lines of sight intersect we have the position of the site that we are looking for. The wider the angle between the alignment of the bearings, the more accurate the result will be.

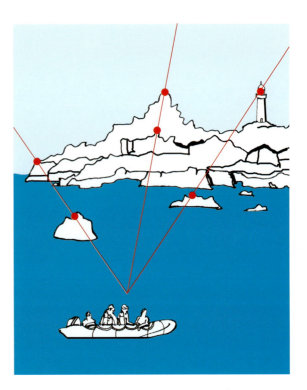

Global Positioning Systems (GPS)

The modern way to locate a dive site that does not have any obvious features above water is to use a Global Positioning System (GPS) receiver. GPS may not be accurate enough to enable divers to locate a small shipwreck but it will provide the means to get them near enough to locate the site with an echo sounder (a device that determines any change in the depth of the seabed by emitting high-frequency sound, and timing how long the sound takes to echo back to the source).

■ There are 24 NAVSTAR satellites in orbit, each transmitting its precise position and correct time. GPS receivers must have a direct line of sight to three or more of these satellites to fix a point. (Fixes from four satellites are preferable because the four fixes enclose a volume of space, rather than converging on a single point.) A civilian GPS receiver can compute its own latitude and longitude down to ± 100m (110 yd).

■ You must remember that any equipment that relies on batteries or electronics can fail, and is also subject to operator error. Before relying on GPS for navigation in remote areas, you must be able to navigate by conventional means.

top THE POSITION OF THE DIVE SITE IS WHERE THE BEARINGS OF LINES OF SIGHT TO OBVIOUS FIXED FEATURES INTERSECT, AS THIS ILLUSTRATION SHOWS.
above GPS RECEIVERS HAVE REVOLUTIONIZED THE TASK OF LOCATING DIVE LOCATIONS THAT ARE BEYOND THE SIGHT OF LAND.

PRE-DIVE BRIEFINGS ARE A SOURCE OF IMPORTANT INFORMATION.

Dive planning
'Plan the dive and dive the plan'

All dives should be planned. The leader of the dive will give a detailed briefing that covers your expected time in the water, what the weather and current are doing, what you should see on the dive, what depth you should expect to dive to and when you should ascend.

However, you should take into account your own health and fitness, your normal rate of air consumption, the depths and times of your last few dives and the surface intervals between those dives and the dive that you are about to perform. You must also think about the dives that you plan to do next. The first dive of the day should always be the deepest and every other dive on that same day should be shallower than the one preceding it.

Dive planners and decompression tables

As it takes time for the body to absorb and release nitrogen, it is possible to dive and return to the surface before the body absorbs enough nitrogen to cause any problems. Back on the surface, excess nitrogen will continue to be released by the body, but if the diver undertakes another dive too soon after the initial dive,

then he or she will commence the subsequent dive with excess nitrogen in his or her body tissues.

Research has established safe time limits (no-stop times) for any given depth where the diver's risk of DCS is minimized. These limits assume that the diver makes a direct ascent (i.e. a square profile dive) at a sensible rate, as ascent itself is a form of decompression.

This research is the basis of the dive planners and decompression tables produced by each dive training agency as a way of calculating the longest time that divers can dive to a given depth and still make a direct ascent; in other words, a no-stop dive. If these times are exceeded, some decompression tables will suggest the depth and duration of any pauses required on the

Did you know?

Because a warm diver has a faster rate of blood circulation and therefore more exchange of nitrogen between the blood and the tissues, diving in warm water increases the chance of suffering DCS.

ascent to enable the release of enough nitrogen for safety (i.e. decompression stops). All dive planners and decompression tables give the fastest rates at which divers should ascend and descend and the shortest time on the surface required for out-gasing nitrogen before diving again (the surface interval). They will also enable you to calculate how your surface interval affects your next dive, due to the estimated amount of nitrogen remaining in your body tissues.

All the major dive training agencies print their own dive planners or decompression tables on plastic cards so that they can be used underwater. They have the same basic functions, but none will guarantee that there is no risk of DCS, as each person is different.

top EACH DIVE TRAINING AGENCY HAS PRODUCED ITS OWN SET OF DIVE PLANNERS, SUCH AS THIS NAUI DIVE PLANNER. RECREATIONAL DIVERS SHOULD ALWAYS USE THE DIVE PLANNERS THEY HAVE BEEN TRAINED WITH.
above A DIVE TIME CALCULATOR ENABLES DIVERS TO CALCULATE NO-STOP TIMES WITH EASE.

Dive planners and decompression tables require that divers have some way of recording the dive time (the amount of time elapsed since they left the surface), the maximum depth reached, the diver's current depth at any given time, and the time spent at any decompression stop indicated.

Once back on the surface, if more dives are to be performed that day or in the next 16 hours, then as well as timing the surface interval, divers must use a dive planner or decompression tables to work out a surfacing code, which estimates how much excess nitrogen remains in the body. By combining this with the surface interval, divers can work out which table to use for the next dive. If times or depths fall between figures on the tables, use the largest figure shown.

Special tables, or sections of existing tables, are designed specifically for diving at altitude and for diving on Enriched Air Nitrox (EAN).

Repetitive dives

For surface intervals of greater than 16 hours, divers can assume that there is no excess nitrogen remaining and treat the next dive as if it were the first. However, a second, or subsequent, dive in less than a 16-hour period must be classed as a repetitive dive. In this case, the possible depths and maximum times can be easily calculated from the dive planner or dive tables but the maximum depth of each subsequent dive must always be shallower than that of the previous dive.

Modern recreational dive planners and dive tables allow divers to perform several repetitive dives in one day, while the British Royal Navy and US Navy tables allow for only two dives in 24 hours.

If you are making repetitive dives over several days, you should take one complete day off after four days to allow any nitrogen remaining in your body tissues to dissipate completely.

Decompression dives

Recreational divers should not make decompression dives, and most American recreational dive planners do not allow for them, although European dive tables do. However, there may be times when for some reason a diver has exceeded the no-stop dive time limit at a given depth. If this happens, the diver must make decompression stops on the ascent for long enough to let excess nitrogen diffuse out of the body tissues.

Different agencies recommend different depths and times for these stops. If the diver has not been very deep and not for too long, then only one stop will be required, usually between 3m and 6m (10–20ft) below the surface. If the diver has been relatively deep or exceeded the no-stop time for longer, he or she will have to make additional stops at deeper depths and then a longer one between 3m and 6m (10–20ft). If a swell is lifting the diver up and down, it is often easier to maintain a stop in deeper water than one closer to the surface.

If you are planning to make a final dive late in the day (such as a night dive), it would be wise to limit this to a depth no greater than 6m (20ft) as this would not be considered as increasing your nitrogen loading.

DIVERS FINISHING OFF A DIVE WITH A FIVE-MINUTE SAFETY STOP.

Finishing a dive

All dives, whether non-decompression or decompression, should be finished with a five-minute safety stop between 3m and 6m (10–20ft). In rough conditions or a swell, when it can be difficult to hold to a stop at 3m (10ft), it is easier to stop at 5m (16ft) as this allows some leeway if the swell causes you to ascend a little.

Altitude and flying after diving

Most decompression model calculations are based on ascending to the atmospheric pressure found at sea level. If you are diving at altitude (in an inland lake, for instance), this must be allowed for with tables or computers designed for altitude diving.

If you fly before the body has had enough time to release most of the extra nitrogen it has absorbed, the reduced pressure in aircraft cabins could cause large bubbles to form. Current medical opinion suggests waiting 24 hours before flying after no-stop diving or 48 hours following a dive requiring decompression stops.

Diving computers

Diving computers save time spent working out dive times from conventional dive planners or decompression tables. They are particularly useful when checking for a suitable dive profile for your next dive, diving more than twice a day or diving with mixed gases. Some diving computers can automatically recognize the salinity of the water while others are calibrated either for sea water or for fresh water.

Many manufacturers also include information supplied by most other diving instruments, with the exception of the compass. Some diving computers are air-integrated, connecting to the first stage high-pressure port either through a high-pressure hose or by a hoseless transducer, enabling an estimate to be made of the amount of air remaining at the diver's current depth and current consumption rate. Diving computers measure time and depth and relate these to decompression tables or 'tissue models' (the rate at which nitrogen might be absorbed or released from solution in the body tissues) to calculate decompression or no-decompression times.

top left INTEGRATED DEPTH GAUGE AND COMPASS. top right MODERN DIVING COMPUTER. bottom CONSOLE CONTAINING A MODERN COMPUTER AND A COMPASS. MAKE SURE THAT THE DIGITS ON YOUR INSTRUMENTS ARE LARGE ENOUGH FOR YOU TO READ.

Hints for computer-assisted diving

Buy a diving computer with displays that are large enough for you to read easily underwater and simple enough to understand when you have mild nitrogen narcosis or are stressed, as this is not the time to be trying to understand ambiguous figures or icons.

Do not pay expensively for a protective cover for your diving computer display. Clear self-adhesive vehicle-type masking tape is tough, waterproof and easily replaced.

A diving computer that switches itself on in 1m (3ft) of water will eliminate any chance of you forgetting to switch it on. Buy a computer that emits an audible warning whenever you violate the rules of diving. However, if it is mounted on your wrist, do not wave your arms about or the unit will assume that you are ascending too fast and react with audible warnings.

As underwater photographers usually have their hands full with photographic equipment, making it difficult to pick up and read computers that are fitted into consoles, they will find that a wrist-mounted unit is more convenient to read. A back-light feature is useful for dim light, wreck, night or cave diving.

Equipment manufacturers use different algorithms, so if your buddy's computer quotes different times, use the times given by your own. The computer takes into account your total nitrogen loading over many dives, but they may not all have been with the same buddy.

Do not dive to the computer's limits, and remember that your chances of developing decompression sickness increase with poor circulation, exertion, dehydration, cold, drugs (including alcohol and caffeine) and poor physical fitness.

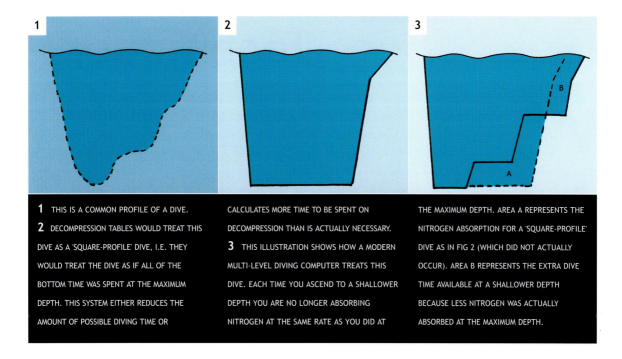

1 THIS IS A COMMON PROFILE OF A DIVE.

2 DECOMPRESSION TABLES WOULD TREAT THIS DIVE AS A 'SQUARE-PROFILE' DIVE, I.E. THEY WOULD TREAT THE DIVE AS IF ALL OF THE BOTTOM TIME WAS SPENT AT THE MAXIMUM DEPTH. THIS SYSTEM EITHER REDUCES THE AMOUNT OF POSSIBLE DIVING TIME OR CALCULATES MORE TIME TO BE SPENT ON DECOMPRESSION THAN IS ACTUALLY NECESSARY.

3 THIS ILLUSTRATION SHOWS HOW A MODERN MULTI-LEVEL DIVING COMPUTER TREATS THIS DIVE. EACH TIME YOU ASCEND TO A SHALLOWER DEPTH YOU ARE NO LONGER ABSORBING NITROGEN AT THE SAME RATE AS YOU DID AT THE MAXIMUM DEPTH. AREA A REPRESENTS THE NITROGEN ABSORPTION FOR A 'SQUARE-PROFILE' DIVE AS IN FIG 2 (WHICH DID NOT ACTUALLY OCCUR). AREA B REPRESENTS THE EXTRA DIVE TIME AVAILABLE AT A SHALLOWER DEPTH BECAUSE LESS NITROGEN WAS ACTUALLY ABSORBED AT THE MAXIMUM DEPTH.

Diving computers are not infallible, however, as they are calculated on mathematical algorithms based on research with fit young men. Some diving computers make allowances for cold water and higher than normal rates of exercise but they do not allow for people who are overweight, unfit or over 50. Some allow their owners to adjust their rate of conservatism. Other diving computers are designed to stop supplying information if you go into decompression (these are best avoided as they become unusable when you most need them, such as when you have made a mistake!).

Full-function decompression-stop diving computers supply information on the depths and times of stage-decompression (pauses during ascent) necessary if you have exceeded the limits of no-stop diving.

Battery failure is common, so either carry two diving computers or have one diving computer together with decompression tables, a watch and a depth gauge as backup. (In areas where support is nonexistent, you can easily be let down by batteries; the computers could switch themselves on in humid climates or their batteries might discharge more quickly in the heat. It is worth buying a unit with owner-replaceable batteries and carrying extra batteries in your spares box.)

Most diving computers will allow their owners to scroll through recent dive data to recall information for their logbook, but some also have the ability to interface with a personal computer (PC). You can then transfer your previous dive profiles to disk as a method of maintaining your logbook. This information is also indispensable for doctors if you suffer decompression sickness. Some of the functions of the diving computer can also be altered manually.

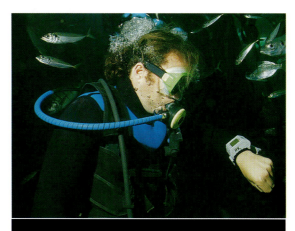

A DIVING COMPUTER ENABLES A DIVER TO MONITOR THE AVAILABLE NO-STOP OR DECOMPRESSION TIME DURING THE COURSE OF THE DIVE.

Safety & Rescue Techniques

With the correct training, scuba diving is a safe sport. There are many physiological situations that could affect a diver, and those specifically related to diving are covered in Diving and the Body (refer to p22). This chapter covers incidents that could happen to anyone anywhere, although they may be more difficult to deal with in the diving environment. All divers should include a recognized course in first aid as part of their basic training.

above WHEN MAKING AN EMERGENCY ASCENT, DIVERS WEARING DRY SUITS MUST RAISE THE ARM CONTAINING DUMP VALVES TO DUMP AIR.

right EXPLORING WRECKS, SUCH AS THIS B17 BOMBER, IS ONE OF THE PLEASURES OF DIVING, PROVIDED YOU OBSERVE SAFETY PRECAUTIONS.

Basic rescue techniques

An unconscious diver is often easier to deal with as he or she is unlikely to be aggressive. A conscious diver in panic can endanger the safety of the rescuer, possibly leading to two casualties rather than one. In these circumstances, monitor the distressed diver from a safe distance until he or she either calms down or becomes sufficiently incapacitated to pose no further threat.

The rescuer should face the casualty so that he or she can easily reach the controls of both his or her and the casualty's BCD inflation and dump valves, weight belt and, if worn, dry suit inflation and dump valves.

Take hold of the casualty in such a way that positive contact can be maintained. However, the casualty's BCD (and dry suit if worn) should be kept more buoyant than that of the rescuer so that if contact is lost the casualty will rise to the surface. (It is better for a casualty to rise to the surface in an uncontrolled manner than not at all.) When inflating the casualty's BCD, the direct feed is easier to use because operating the small emergency cylinder will require two hands.

Buddy Checks

By keeping an eye on each other, one of you should soon notice if the other is behaving in a strange way.

Things to look out for include:

- Stress caused by swimming against a current
- Nervousness
- Rapid breathing
- Signals that the diver is having problems breathing
- Erratic and unco-ordinated movements (convulsions)
- Problems with buoyancy control
- Failure to respond to signals
- Wide, staring eyes
- Vigorously treading water
- Inactivity

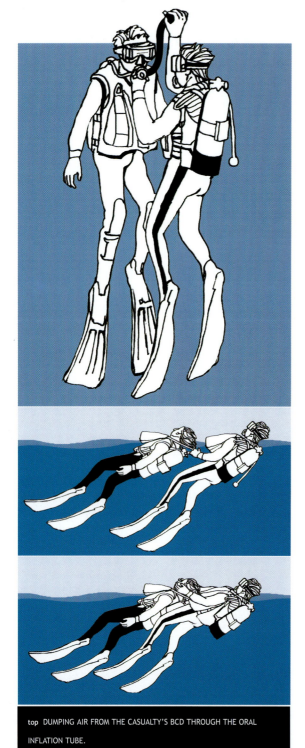

top DUMPING AIR FROM THE CASUALTY'S BCD THROUGH THE ORAL INFLATION TUBE.

middle A CONSCIOUS CASUALTY CAN BE TOWED BY GRIPPING A CONVENIENT PART OF HIS EQUIPMENT, WHILE AN UNCONSCIOUS CASUALTY (bottom) NEEDS AN ADEQUATE NECK EXTENSION DURING THE TOW. THIS WILL REQUIRE TWO HANDS.

Make sure that you do not ascend faster than the smallest bubbles. If the ascent rate becomes too fast you will have to vent some air from both your own and the casualty's BCD or dry suit. If both of you have dry suits with wrist-mounted dump valves, you will have to raise each of the arms with these valves.

However, you may be holding the casualty's left arm with your right arm, or vice versa, and one of you may not have a dump valve on the arm concerned. As you cannot raise all four arms or you could lose contact, the correct procedure is to raise your own arm that has the dump valve, but to dump air from the casualty's dry suit by simply inserting a finger beneath the wrist seal of the casualty's raised arm.

You can vent air from both of your BCDs through their dump valves but it may be easier to dump air from the casualty's BCD through the large corrugated oral-inflation tube by raising the tube and depressing its purge button. The casualty may not have enough air left to achieve buoyancy with his or her BCD or dry suit. In this situation try to lift him or her by inflating your own BCD, but if this does not work, ditch the casualty's weight belt and try again.

As you ascend make sure that you breathe out yourself and depress the casualty's stomach to try to make him or her breathe out. Once on the surface, inflate the casualty's BCD enough to give buoyancy but not so much that you cannot give exhaled air resuscitation (EAR), also known as mouth to mouth (refer to p78), if necessary. Do not inflate a dry suit if worn.

If the casualty has to be towed, both the rescuer and casualty should be on their backs. A conscious casualty should be towed from behind, with the rescuer holding on to any convenient item of the casualty's equipment, such as a BCD shoulder strap.

An unconscious casualty will require a clear airway, so tow him or her by gripping the point of the chin to keep the head back. In a rough sea you will also have to place your other hand under the neck for support.

If you are faced with a long tow, then ditch the casualty's weight belt and scuba cylinder, but keep your own weight belt on as it will keep your legs lower in the water and make finning more efficient.

THE BASIC PRINCIPLES are to:
- Preserve life
- Prevent the condition from worsening
- Promote recovery.

In the event of an accident we should do the minimum necessary to achieve these objectives while transporting the casualty to more qualified medical aid.

The first things to check are the ABCs:

A is for AIRWAY
B is for BREATHING
C is for CIRCULATION
D is for DECREASED LEVEL OF CONSCIOUSNESS
E is for EXPOSURE

The first thing to do is to ensure both the casualty's and rescuer's safety by removing them from danger, but make sure that by doing this you do not damage the casualty further. (For instance, if the casualty is not breathing it may be necessary to give EAR in the water first.)

Airway

Is there any injury to the neck or obstruction to the mouth or nose? Noisy breathing could indicate an obstructed airway.

Breathing

Is the chest rising and falling? Listen for movement of air in the nose and mouth. Can you feel air moving against your hand or cheek?

Circulation

Can you feel a pulse next to the windpipe (the carotid artery)?

Decreased level of consciousness

Does the casualty respond in any of the following ways (use 'AVPU' to help you remember):
A: Is the casualty awake, aware, or capable of speech?
V: Verbal stimuli — does the casualty answer to 'WAKE UP'?
P: Painful stimuli — does the casualty respond to a slap, pinch or pin prick?
U: Is the casualty unresponsive?

Exposure

Is the casualty too hot or too cold? Cover with a blanket or warm clothing, or provide shade. Remove any clothing necessary to give adequate treatment, but preserve the casualty's dignity at all times.

If you think the casualty's condition is serious, send or call for help from the emergency services (ambulance, paramedics, etc.). If you send someone to call for help, that person must come back to confirm that help is on the way.

The recovery position

If the casualty is breathing but unconscious, the recovery position is a stable position that ensures there is an adequate airway. Any vomit will drain away so that the casualty does not choke. The casualty should never be left alone and should be continually monitored for any change in his or her condition.

IN THE RECOVERY POSITION THE CASUALTY ALWAYS HAS AN ADEQUATE AIRWAY, CANNOT ROLL OVER ONTO HIS OR HER BACK AND ANY VOMIT WILL DRAIN AWAY.

Exhaled air resuscitation

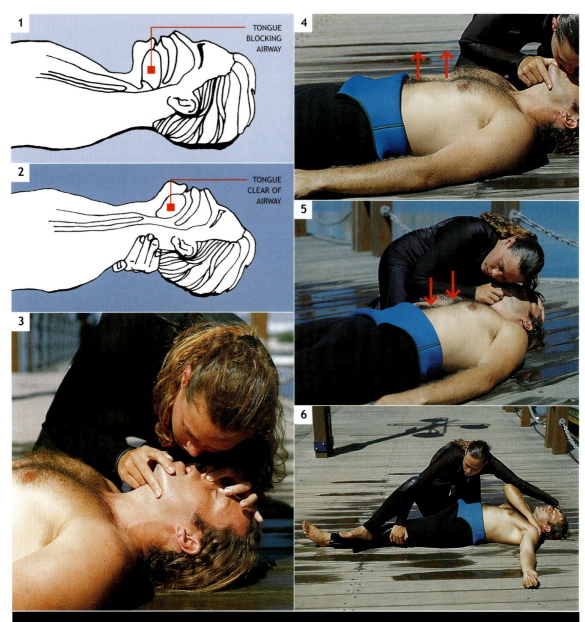

THERE IS A SIMPLE SEQUENCE TO EXHALED AIR RESUSCITATION (EAR OR MOUTH TO MOUTH) AND LEARNING IT CAN SAVE LIVES.

1 IN THE NORMAL POSITION OF THE NECK WHEN LYING DOWN, THE TONGUE MAY BLOCK THE AIRWAY.

2 CLEAR THE AIRWAY BY RAISING THE CASUALTY'S NECK.

3 TILT THE CASUALTY'S HEAD BACK AND ENSURE THAT NOTHING IS BLOCKING THE MOUTH OR AIRWAY, THEN PINCH THE CASUALTY'S NOSE CLOSED BEFORE PLACING YOUR MOUTH OVER HIS OR HER MOUTH AND EXHALING INTO IT. (ALTERNATIVELY, PLACE YOUR HAND OVER THE CASUALTY'S MOUTH TO CLOSE IT, THEN PLACE YOUR MOUTH OVER THE CASUALTY'S NOSE AND EXHALE INTO IT.)

4-5 THE CASUALTY'S CHEST WILL RISE AS YOU EXHALE INTO IT. PAUSE TO TAKE A BREATH AND WATCH TO SEE THAT THE CASUALTY'S CHEST FALLS.

6 TO GET THE CASUALTY INTO THE RECOVERY POSITION, FOLD THE ARM AND LEG CLOSEST TO YOU ACROSS THE BODY, SUPPORT THE HEAD AND USE YOUR OTHER ARM TO ROLL THE CASUALTY AWAY FROM YOU.

EAR on the surface

Where it would take time to reach your surface cover or entry point, you may have to perform exhaled air resuscitation (EAR) on the surface while still in the water.

To do this, partially inflate the casualty's BCD and remove his or her mask. Grip the point of the chin with one hand and lever against the shoulder with your elbow as shown in the diagram below. The neck can then be extended to clear the airway. It is important that you lever against the point of the chin and not the casualty's throat or windpipe.

For EAR in the water you have to use the mouth-to-nose method to achieve a good seal. Place your free hand underneath the casualty's far shoulder and push upward so that his or her body rolls towards you, making it easier for you to reach the nose with your mouth. As the casualty rolls over, allow the arm extending the casualty's neck to move with him or her, by folding it across your chest.

Keep the casualty's mouth sealed, place your own mouth over his or her nose and exhale to inflate the lungs. On completing the inflation of the casualty's lungs, let him or her roll back into the normal floating position. This is very tiring for the rescuer, but try to make four inflations of the casualty's lungs before taking a rest.

Cardiopulmonary resuscitation

There is no point in continuing EAR if the casualty's heart is not beating, because the oxygenated blood will not be pumped around the body. Check to see whether the heart is beating by feeling for a pulse at the carotid artery in the neck.

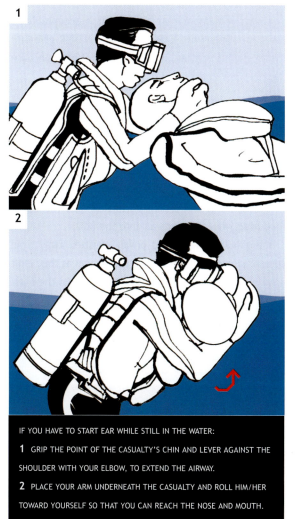

IF YOU HAVE TO START EAR WHILE STILL IN THE WATER:

1 GRIP THE POINT OF THE CASUALTY'S CHIN AND LEVER AGAINST THE SHOULDER WITH YOUR ELBOW, TO EXTEND THE AIRWAY.

2 PLACE YOUR ARM UNDERNEATH THE CASUALTY AND ROLL HIM/HER TOWARD YOURSELF SO THAT YOU CAN REACH THE NOSE AND MOUTH.

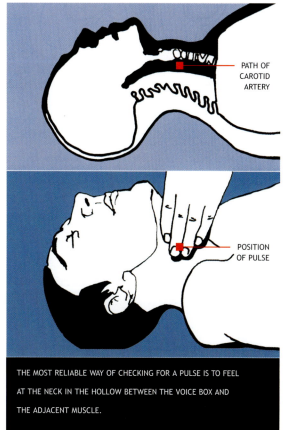

PATH OF CAROTID ARTERY

POSITION OF PULSE

THE MOST RELIABLE WAY OF CHECKING FOR A PULSE IS TO FEEL AT THE NECK IN THE HOLLOW BETWEEN THE VOICE BOX AND THE ADJACENT MUSCLE.

If you cannot feel a pulse, then the casualty will require cardiopulmonary resuscitation (CPR). This compresses the casualty's heart between the breastbone and the spine, forcing the blood to circulate. Then when you release the pressure, the heart expands again, drawing in more blood which is expelled by the next compression.

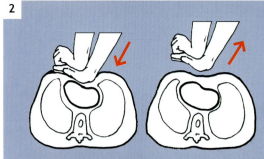

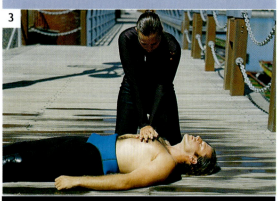

1 BEFORE STARTING CPR, FEEL FOR A PULSE AT THE CAROTID ARTERY.

2 - 3 MEASURE TWO FINGER WIDTHS ABOVE THE NOTCH WHERE THE RIBS MEET THE LOWER END OF THE BREASTBONE. PLACE THE HEEL OF YOUR LEFT HAND OVER THIS SPOT AND PLACE THE HEEL OF YOUR RIGHT HAND OVER YOUR LEFT HAND. STRAIGHTEN YOUR ELBOWS AND ROCK FORWARD IN A JERKY MOTION TO COMPRESS THE BREASTBONE BY 5CM (2IN). TO ACHIEVE THE CORRECT RATE, COUNT 'ONE AND TWO AND THREE' AND SO ON.

To begin CPR, place the casualty face up on a hard surface and kneel alongside him or her. Measure two finger widths above the notch where the ribs meet the lower end of the breastbone. Place the heel of your left hand over this spot and place the heel of your right hand over your left hand. Straighten your elbows and rock forward in a jerky motion to compress the breastbone by 5cm (2in). To achieve the correct rhythm, count the compressions at a rate of 'one and two and three' etc.

Complete 15 compressions at the rate of 80 per minute and then give two EAR exhalations and check the pulse. Continue to give a sequence of 15 CPR compressions followed by two EAR exhalations and a check on the pulse. If the heart starts, it is essential that you cease giving CPR.

Always remember that although it is acceptable to assist breathing with EAR, you should NEVER give CPR if the heart is beating, no matter how faintly, because the rhythmic action of the heart is easily upset.

Rescue equipment
Power whistles

Power whistles are much more effective than oral whistles at attracting your boat cover. Also called air horns, power whistles are powered by low-pressure compressed air, and are fitted in line with the direct feed hose where it feeds air into the BCD.

You should always hold power whistles away from yourself and other divers when using them as they emit a very loud noise which could be damaging to the ears.

POWER WHISTLES ARE EXTREMELY EFFECTIVE IN ATTRACTING BOAT COVER, PARTICULARLY WHEN WAVES MAKE VISIBILITY DIFFICULT.

Dive flags

The official flag that covers both professional and sport diving is the maritime International Code of Signals 'A' flag. When flown on its own, the 'A' flag signifies that a vessel has divers in the water so other craft should keep clear and reduce speed. It is illegal to fly this flag if the vessel concerned does not actually have divers in the water at the time the flag is displayed.

American recreational divers have produced their own diving flag; this one does not have any legal international meaning and will often be flown outside diving establishments and on vessels that do not have divers in the water. Some diving operators or shops add their own logo to this flag.

surface marker buoys, so check local regulations before taking to the water. SMBs can be augmented with flashing 'strobe lights' for night diving or in poor visibility.

Ideally only one diver of a buddy pair or the leader of a group diving together should display an SMB as the lines are easily tangled up if several are used. However, each individual diver should carry a delayed deployment SMB in case the divers become separated. Deflated and rolled up in a BCD pocket, delayed deployment SMBs may take the form of 'rescue sausages', highly visible orange tubes about 1.5m (5ft) long that are closed at the top end and are either open at the base for inflation by your regulator second stage or have an oral inflation valve. The open-base type

THE INTERNATIONALLY RECOGNIZED 'A' FLAG SIGNIFIES THAT A BOAT HAS DIVERS IN THE WATER.

AMERICAN DIVERS HAVE THEIR OWN FLAG. ALTHOUGH IT HAS NO LEGAL STATUS, IT IS WIDELY USED BY DIVING OPERATORS.

Surface marker buoys

The surface marker buoy (SMB) is a highly visible float, sometimes incorporating a dive flag, that is connected to the diver by a thin strong line wound around a reel to enable it to be easily reeled out on descent and reeled in on ascent.

The main function of SMBs is to let the surface boat cover know where the divers are at all times and provide a means by which the boat crew can communicate with the divers (by jerking it sharply). SMBs can be very useful when diving in strong currents, choppy seas, poor visibility or when swimming out from the shore. In places where jet-skis, water skiers, pleasure and commercial boats are active, it may be law for divers to use

must be inflated underwater. Most SMBs, including all the tube types, have a small sinker weight attached to their base to help them to float in the upright position.

Every diver's worst nightmare is surfacing in heavy seas with the boat cover a long way off or out of sight. Apart from SMBs you can carry either manual or compressed air whistles (power whistles) and waterproof flares or dye markers that colour a large enough area of water to be seen from the air. If you are diving in a country where air search is possible, there are waterproof emergency radio beacons similar to those used by yachtsmen. It is important that divers in this predicament remain together, so tie yourselves together with a buddy line if the waves or current are strong.

Types of Diving

One of the attractions of diving is its variety. Depending on your fitness you can take a gentle swim or opt for a high-voltage drift dive in a strong current. Some divers prefer clear, warm water with spectacular reefs, while others are happy with kelp forests and the limited visibility found in colder waters.

Once you are qualified there are several routes that you can take to enhance your diving. Many divers take additional courses, such as underwater photography, wreck diving or search and rescue techniques, while others opt to become dive leaders or divemasters in order to share their love of the sport with others.

Even if you only wish to dive for your own pleasure there are numerous specialist courses that will lead you towards becoming an advanced diver. Another option is to take courses that will enable you to become an internationally qualified scuba diving instructor with the possibility of working around the world, or eventually running your own dive operation.

Temperate vs tropical waters

Many divers perform most of their diving in temperate (cool) waters, where the fish and invertebrate life can be just as interesting as in most tropical waters though not always as colourful. Generally the visibility and surface conditions will not always be that good in cold water. To cope with this environment, exposure suits must be in good condition and divers should be both well trained and fit. In temperate waters, shipwrecks are often the most popular dive sites.

By contrast, when diving in the warm, clear waters of the tropics, surrounded by a variety of marine life, you are likely to be more relaxed. The main danger with such clear water is that you are likely to dive deeper than you are accustomed to without realizing it. Many of the more popular diving holiday destinations are in areas where tides and currents are minimal and sea conditions are usually calm.

Even in warm water, it is wise to wear thin exposure suits as protection against creatures that sting, but the biggest chance of ruining your holiday comes from sunburn or insect bites when you are not diving.

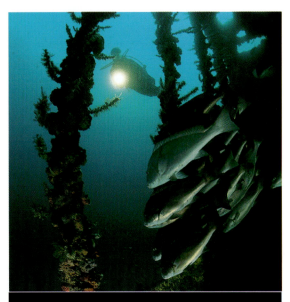

above SHIPWRECKS ARE POPULAR DIVE SITES IN TEMPERATE WATERS.

above BRIGHT SPONGES ARE A TYPICAL FEATURE OF TROPICAL WATERS.

right QUALIFIED DIVERS HAVE A VARIETY OF ENVIRONMENTS TO EXPLORE.

Diving from a day boat

THERE IS AMPLE ROOM TO MOVE around on a day boat and scuba cylinders will be contained in special racks, so you can leave your kitting-up until you are 15 minutes from the dive site.

Entry into the water is the same as entry from a jetty, that is, either a forward roll or a long stride entry (refer to p65).

In strong currents there should be a floating line clear of the ladder, which divers already in the water can hold onto while waiting for their buddies.

Exiting the water is up steps or a ladder and how you manage this will depend on sea conditions. Where the sea is calm, remove your fins and pass them to some-

one onboard before climbing the ladder. If the sea is rough, keep your fins on, because if a wave throws you back into the water, you will find you cannot swim effectively while wearing a BCD and scuba cylinder but not fins.

Climbing a ladder on a rocking boat when you are wearing fins and full scuba equipment is

top PREPARING FOR A DIVE IN BONAIRE, IN THE DUTCH CARIBBEAN, DIVERS SIGN ON AND STOW THEIR CYLINDERS SECURELY IN THE RACKS.

above DAY BOATS MOORED OVER THE WRECK OF THE *JOLANDA* AT SHARK REEF IN THE RED SEA.

difficult so it is worth practising in calm conditions. Some boats have single pole ladders (a central pole with steps on either side), which are much easier to climb while wearing fins than a conventional runged ladder.

When a boat is not moored or at anchor, divers have little chance of reaching it if it is being moved away from them by the wind or currents. In these circumstances, the coxswain (helmsman) should motor the boat until it is upwind of the divers, then disengage the engine and let the boat drift downwind toward the divers.

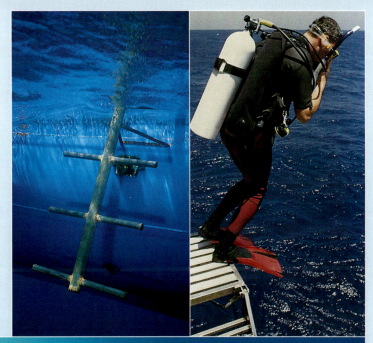

top left A SINGLE POLE LADDER IS EASIER TO CLIMB WHEN WEARING FINS.

top right AT ELPHINSTONE REEF IN THE RED SEA A DIVER HOLDS ONTO HIS MASK AND MOUTHPIECE BEFORE LEAPING INTO THE WATER.

above BEGINNING A DIVE AT TAVEUNI IN THE FIJI ISLANDS. DAY BOATS ENABLE DIVERS TO EXPLORE MANY DIVE SITES FROM A CENTRAL LOCATION.

LIVE-ABOARD DIVING HAS several advantages over shore-based and day boat diving. There is less carrying of heavy equipment, no long swims over shallow fringing reefs, and in particular, live-aboards mean that divers are able to reach remote offshore reefs and wrecks. There are usually also fewer restrictions on night dives and divers can get three to five dives each day instead of heading back to shore after one or two.

Live-aboards may appear expensive, but you get more dives for your money and all food is included. On the minus side, some boats are too narrow or too high in the water, so they roll about uncomfortably at the slightest hint of a rough sea.

To enter the water from a live-aboard boat, you may be close enough to the dive site to leap into the water as you would off a jetty, but it is more likely that you will use either a tender (dinghy or small inflatable boat) to reach the dive sites.

Most divers do not like to have large numbers of people in the water at the same time. Bigger live-aboard boats should either have two tenders serving two separate dive sites simultane-ously, or have a system whereby only half their clients are in the water at any one time, while the other half are resting.

Although live-aboard boats frequently offer up to five dives each day, divers also have to consider tides and currents, and other dives that have been performed or are planned for that day. (Refer to tides and currents p62 and repetitive dives p70.)

In areas where the tidal range is high there will be times when the current is too strong for comfortable diving.

Similarly, when a tide is flowing off a reef or the land (ebb tide), the visibility will be poor. In these situations it would

top LIVE-ABOARD BOATS VARY ENORMOUSLY IN DESIGN AND FACILITIES, AND THE COST AND COMFORT LEVELS VARY ACCORDINGLY, SO CHOOSE AN OPERATOR THAT MEETS YOUR NEEDS.

above THE ATTRACTIONS OF DIVING IN-OUT-OF-THE-WAY, OFTEN UNSPOILT, LOCATIONS MAKE LIVE-ABOARDS AN OPTION FOR THE ADVENTUROUS DIVER.

be better to make fewer dives each day but pick the right times in the tide tables to have interesting, quality dives, rather than having five dives on each day where some of them are likely to be mediocre ones.

Silent entry

When you wish to approach a fish or other marine creature without scaring it into flight, a silent entry is called for.

From a large boat you should climb down the ladder, but from a smaller boat you should turn onto your stomach and lower yourself gently into the water over the side of the boat, taking care that your equipment and fins do not splash as you enter.

top DIVERS SORT OUT THEIR GEAR AND KIT-UP BEFORE A DIVE IN THE RED SEA.

above FROM A LIVE-ABOARD BOAT YOU WOULD NORMALLY CLIMB DOWN INTO A TENDER, SIT TO ONE SIDE AND THEN PUT ON YOUR FINS BEFORE BEING TAKEN TO THE DIVE SITE.

Drift diving

Drift diving can vary from pleasantly drifting along a wall in a gentle current to high-voltage rushes as you are swept along walls and gullies, with the possibility of spotting large pelagic species.

The main problems on a drift dive are those of good boat cover and becoming separated from your buddy or group. If you are not using a surface marker buoy (SMB), then at least carry a high-visibility orange rescue tube or collapsible flag, both of which can be raised above the swell, to be more visible to the boat cover. Power whistles are better at attracting your boat cover than manual whistles. (Refer to power whistles p80.)

Buddies, and preferably the whole group, should enter the water together so that they do not get separated on the surface, and should try to keep together underwater.

If you do get separated from your boat cover, it is wise to tie a line between yourself and your buddy, inflate your BCD and conserve air in case you subsequently have to make a difficult exit through surf or foaming breakers. It is usually best to retain your weight belt unless buoyancy is a problem (in some circumstances it may be better to jettison your scuba cylinders).

If you wish to fin ashore and are wearing a normal BCD rather than wings, it is less tiring to fin on your back. Untie the buddy line before swimming through surf.

Night diving

Night is a time of change. Dusk and dawn are the times when predators are most active, as they can rise unseen out of the darkness to take prey made visible against the lighter sky.

Night diving can be fraught with anxiety at first, as visibility is reduced to the narrow beam provided by your underwater light, shadows move ominously and

IN A DRIFT DIVE, ONE DIVER WILL OFTEN TOW A SURFACE MARKER BUOY TO ENABLE THE BOAT COVER TO FOLLOW THE PROGRESS OF THE GROUP.

noises seem amplified, but you will soon relax. Many fish hide in crevices or under the sand but some fish and many invertebrates (creatures that do not have a backbone), prefer to feed at night.

What you are likely to see on a night dive depends on the time. Dusk, when there is still plenty of light above water, is good for watching predators hunting, while diving between 7 and 9pm (19:00 and 21:00) would enable you to see most of the interesting night creatures. To be sure of catching parrot fish in their cocoons you should dive after 10pm (22:00).

When planning a night dive, choose an area with little wave and current action and easily recognizable features for navigation, and dive the area first during daylight to familiarize yourself with the topography. When setting out at night, mark your designated point of exit with a light. Start the dive by swimming against the current and return with it.

Avoid lights that are too bright and always carry a second light for backup as underwater lights are notorious for failing. (Rechargeable lights powered by nickel-cadmium batteries give out without warning, so use alkaline batteries in your backup light.)

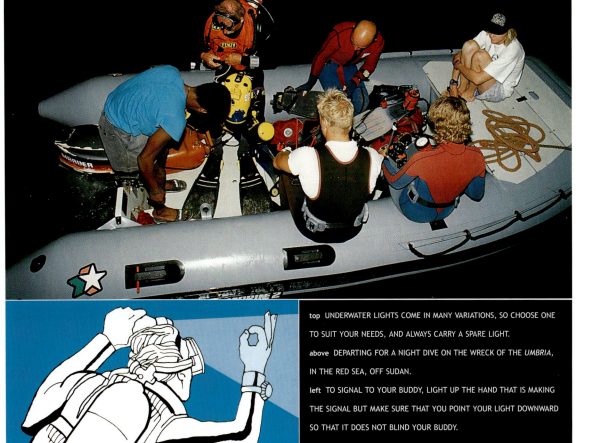

top UNDERWATER LIGHTS COME IN MANY VARIATIONS, SO CHOOSE ONE TO SUIT YOUR NEEDS, AND ALWAYS CARRY A SPARE LIGHT.

above DEPARTING FOR A NIGHT DIVE ON THE WRECK OF THE *UMBRIA*, IN THE RED SEA, OFF SUDAN.

left TO SIGNAL TO YOUR BUDDY, LIGHT UP THE HAND THAT IS MAKING THE SIGNAL BUT MAKE SURE THAT YOU POINT YOUR LIGHT DOWNWARD SO THAT IT DOES NOT BLIND YOUR BUDDY.

Wreck diving

Wreck diving is one of the most popular forms of diving but it requires care as wrecks can break up unexpectedly or be snagged by fishing lines or nets.

Choose slack water, carry a good light plus an additional backup light, cut-through-anything shears for your equipment is tucked away against your body so that it will not snag anywhere. If you intend to enter a wreck, tie off a lifeline before entering and feed it out as you go. It will enable you to find your way out again if you become disoriented as the sediment is stirred up. Remember that your fins and hands, as well as your

DIVERS EXPLORING WRECKS SHOULD ALWAYS CARRY A SHARP KNIFE, AN ADDITIONAL BACKUP LIGHT AND A PAIR OF SHEARS. ENTERING WRECKS CAN BE DANGEROUS AND IS NOT FOR THE INEXPERIENCED.

cutting monofilament fishing line or nets, and a sharp knife. Most divers store their diving knife by strapping it to one of their legs, but in this position it can be dislodged by the lifeline or tangled up in fishing lines or nets. It is a good idea to have a separate smaller knife attached to one arm or in the BCD pocket where it is easily reached.

The first pair of divers onto the wreck should tie a shotline (marker line) to the wreck and the final pair of divers to ascend should release it. Make sure that all exhaust bubbles, can disturb sediment. Leave yourself plenty of air to get out again, and secure in an open position all doors and hatches that you pass through so that they cannot close on you in a current. Wrecks sunk specifically for divers should have been environmentally cleaned and all doors and hatches removed.

SOME FRESHWATER SITES ARE FED BY HOT OR COLD SPRINGS, RESULTING IN DIFFERENT TYPES OF UNDERWATER ECOLOGY.

CAVE DIVING DEMANDS EXCEPTIONAL PLANNING AND TREBLING OF EQUIPMENT. NOVICES MUST NEVER ENTER CAVES UNACCOMPANIED.

Freshwater diving

The only difference between diving in sea water and fresh water is that fresh water is less buoyant, more likely to carry parasites that may lead to an infection, and there will not be charts for most freshwater sites.

Some freshwater sites will be at a high enough altitude to require the use of special dive tables and corrections to the measured depths. Heavy rain can often reduce freshwater visibility to zero, and could also lead to flash floods or a rapidly rising water level. In areas where the lakes or rivers are fed by hot springs, be careful as they can get very hot!

Diving in shallow lakes is relatively easy but diving in rivers can be difficult if they are fast flowing. In general the current will be slower near to the riverbank due to the friction of the water against the bank. Before you enter a river you must also consider where you can exit it. One way to move against the current in a river is to use hooks to get a purchase on the bottom so that you can pull yourself along.

Cave diving

The type of cave diving taught on speciality courses prepares you for penetrating a short distance into caverns. The courses teach you how to plan your dive, how to carry scuba cylinders mounted at your side and how to treble up on all your equipment in case of failure. Most importantly you learn how to lay a lifeline and attach direction indicators to it so that you can find your way back out of cave passages in zero visibility. This type of cave diving is within the realm of most recreational divers, but novices should never enter a cave unless accompanied by an experienced cave diver.

By contrast, in exploratory cave diving, the divers involved are cavers first and dive as a means to extend their range of caving exploration. Cave penetration of this type can consist of multi-day expeditions, with extended periods spent underwater breathing mixed gases and surfacing only after long and complicated decompression schedules. Only extremely experienced divers should attempt this type of cave diving.

Deep diving

Just how we define deep diving within recreational diving limits varies with each dive training agency. Some agencies quote depths deeper than 30m (100ft), some quote depths beyond 40m (130ft), others depths beyond 50m (165ft). Divers trained by European training agencies consider dives in the 30–50m (100–165ft) range to be feasible for advanced divers.

FOR DEEP DIVING, EXTRA AIR OR NITROX IN CYLINDERS FITTED WITH REGULATORS AND OCTOPUS RIGS SHOULD BE HUNG AT THE INTENDED DECOMPRESSION DEPTHS.

Deep dives require careful planning. Full scuba cylinders fitted with regulators should be hung at the depths of any planned decompression stops and back-up divers should be kitted-up on the support boat. The backup divers should not have dived that day to ensure that they will not have any nitrogen in their tissues if they are called upon to help the divers in the water.

Diving beyond 50m (165ft) on compressed air is considered hazardous. Commercial divers make deep diving safer by using mixed gases such as Heliox (where helium replaces all of the nitrogen) or Trimix (helium replaces some of the nitrogen). The exact proportions of each gas in the mix are changed according to the requirements of the particular dive plan in order to reduce nitrogen narcosis, oxygen toxicity and the risk of decompression sickness. Some advanced recreational divers have borrowed from the knowledge of commercial divers and applied it to dives beyond 50m (165ft), but diving in this way requires considerable planning over gas mixtures and schedules.

Enriched Air Nitrox

While only a minority of highly trained divers use mixed gases, a big advance for recreational divers is the widespread availability of Enriched Air Nitrox (EAN).

Like air, Enriched Air Nitrox is made up of nitrogen and oxygen, but by increasing the percentage of oxygen the amount of nitrogen has been reduced. EANx32, or Nitrox 32, contains 32% oxygen and 68% nitrogen. (EANx is the standard way of signifying Enriched Air Nitrox and the 'x' denotes the percentage of oxygen in the Nitrox mix.)

By reducing the nitrogen content of their air, divers get longer bottom times for diving without decompression stops or, if they do have to make decompression stops, these will be shorter when using EAN in conjunction with an Enriched Air Nitrox dive computer or decompression tables.

Experienced divers can also use Enriched Air Nitrox in another way; if they breathe EAN but use decompression tables designed for air or a diving computer set for air, they will get a greater safety margin because the table or computer assumes they are breathing 79% nitrogen. Divers also feel less fatigued after Enriched Air Nitrox dives and many experience a lower rate of gas consumption.

However, because of the larger amount of oxygen being breathed with EAN there is an increased risk of oxygen toxicity at depth. The depths that you can dive to are dependent on the percentage of oxygen in the gas mixes being used; the higher the percentage of oxygen used, the shallower you will be able to dive safely. Divers should not dive to a depth where the partial pressure of oxygen exceeds 1.4ata.

There may be circumstances where a diver breathing Enriched Air Nitrox has to go deeper than oxygen toxicity allows on the Nitrox mixture they are breathing.

NITROX CYLINDERS ARE ALWAYS CLEARLY MARKED AND SHOULD NEVER BE REFILLED WITH COMPRESSED AIR OR ANY OTHER GAS.

REBREATHERS WERE ORIGINALLY DEVELOPED FOR MILITARY USE. THEY PROLONG BOTTOM TIME BY RECYCLING EXHALED AIR.

In this situation, if the diver has a separate small cylinder of normal air fitted with its own regulator, he or she can switch to breathing from this cylinder for a brief foray deeper than the depth allowed on the Nitrox mixture that they have been breathing. Then they can switch back to breathing Enriched Air Nitrox once they have returned to a depth where oxygen toxicity is no longer a problem.

Another way in that Enriched Air Nitrox can be used to advantage is to have a smaller cylinder fitted with its own regulator and containing a much higher percentage of oxygen in the Nitrox mix. This is only used on shallow decompression stops, but in this situation the Enriched Air Nitrox is much more efficient as a decompression gas for removing nitrogen than air.

Nitrox cylinders must be clearly marked, never used for any other gas and be free of lubricants that could ignite on contact with high percentages of oxygen.

Rebreathers

Scuba stands for Self Contained Underwater Breathing Apparatus. As most of the oxygen we take in through the scuba cylinder is breathed out into the water, the system is termed an open-circuit system.

Some companies have developed closed- or semi-closed-circuit scuba equipment, termed rebreathers.

With rebreathers, you breathe a gas mixture containing oxygen and after you have exhaled, the carbon dioxide in your exhaled gases is chemically removed by passing these gases through a soda-lime filter (called a scrubber). Some additional oxygen is then added to the gases cleaned of carbon dioxide and you breathe that gas mixture again.

The closed-circuit system does not dump any gas until you ascend, while the semi-closed-circuit system only dumps a small portion of each breath. In this way you get long diving times out of a relatively small amount of breathing gas, but you must keep a constant eye on your gauges to be sure that everything is working correctly. Rebreathers are usually based on Nitrox but for deeper diving they can be based on Trimix or, occasionally, on Heliox.

The world is full of exciting places to dive, from warm tropical seas to temperate oceans. Once you have qualified, your 'C'—card will be the passport that enables you to enjoy this wonderful sport. Good luck and happy diving!

Appendix — How heat, light and sound travel underwater

THE TRANSFER OF HEAT IN WATER

Conduction, the transfer of heat by direct contact, is very poor in air, hence its use as an insulator in duvets and down clothing. Water is denser than air and conducts heat some 25-times more efficiently. An unclad diver may be quite comfortable in air at 21°C (70°F), but at the same temperature in water, the body will lose heat faster than it can generate it and become cold.

Heat is also transmitted by convection; the water in contact with the diver's body heats up and becomes less dense. If this water is not kept in position by an exposure suit, it will rise as heavier, cooler water replaces it (there is always colder water cooling a diver, even when he or she is not moving about).

THE TRANSFER OF LIGHT IN WATER

Because air, glass and water have different densities, light travels at different speeds in each one of them and will be refracted (bent) as it crosses the interface between each medium unless it hits that boundary at right angles. This causes a false impression of distance by ratio of 4:3 and magnification by one-third according to their actual and apparent distances. If an object is 4m (4yd) away, it will appear to be 3m (3yd) away and one-third larger.

Of all the electromagnetic spectrum (the complete range of electromagnetic radiation from the longest radio waves to the shortest gamma radiation), only a narrow range can be recognized by the human eye. Differences in wavelength within this range are perceived as colours.

When light strikes an object, the object absorbs some wavelengths of the light and reflects others. The eye perceives the colour of the object from the visible wavelengths that are reflected. If all the visible wavelengths are reflected, the eye perceives the colour as white; when very few of the visible wavelengths are reflected, the eye perceives it as black. Some objects are stimulated by shorter wavelengths to emit longer visible wavelengths of light, this is termed fluorescence; apart from its use in diving equipment for maximum visibility, it can be observed in some plankton, anemones and corals at night.

As light penetrates water, its wavelengths are progressively filtered out. The first to go are those with the least energy, the reds in the visible spectrum, then orange and yellow, then green and finally blue. At depth there is little or no visible light to reflect off red, orange and yellow objects, so they appear as grey/black unless divers add their own light from an underwater light or strobe.

While the maximum transparency in clear water is for wave-lengths perceived as blue, suspended matter in the water, both organic and inorganic, causes turbidity, the maximum transparency then shifts to yellow-green.

Even clear water scatters, deflects and polarizes light. This is termed diffusion, and it reduces shadows and contrast. Because it is easier to see objects that stand out against their background, the selective absorption of colours will affect what colours contrast with each other.

THE TRANSFER OF SOUND IN WATER

Sound travels considerably faster and further in water than in air. Lower frequency sounds, such as those emanating from a ship's engines or propellers, can often be heard when the source is not actually within sight.

The diver's hearing is reduced by the effect of water on the eardrums, and the increased speed of the sound confuses the stereophonic reception of human ears. Underwater, sound is conducted to the hearing organs through the bones of the skull rather than through the eardrums as in air. Because of this, the delay between the sound reaching one ear then the other is too short for the ears to differentiate between time and intensity, so the sound is perceived as coming from all directions at once.

Sounds made above the water's surface will not be heard in the water and vice versa. Sound transmission is also affected by differing water temperature, as with a thermocline (a meeting point of two layers of water with different temperatures). Different temperatures on either side of the thermocline also mean different densities. When sound waves cross an interface of different densities they lose energy. If the sound originates in water above the thermocline, it may not be heard easily below it.

Index

Credits and acknowledgements

PUBLISHER'S ACKNOWLEDGEMENTS

The publisher wishes to thank the following people and organizations who have provided invaluable help and assistance: In Cape Town — Duncan Patterson, Butch Kriel and Chris Doyle of Orca Industries; Eric Gobel and Nadine Peterson of Underwaterworld; Simon Chater of the Two Oceans Aquarium; Ian Campbell, Michael Denis and students at Sheer Blue Adventures; Peter Labuschagne and students at Table Bay Diving; the instructors and students at the Dive Junction; John Hattingh, Michelle Petersen, Richard Ducket and Jade Maxwell-Newton of Dive Action; Mark Engledow of Scuba Shack; Phil and Melanie Wright for the loan of the rebreather and Messrs Hunter and Hendriks of the Sea Point Swimming Pool. Thanks also to Gary Greenstone for his time and patience on numerous modelling shoots.

PHOTOGRAPHIC CREDITS

All photographs by **Danja Kohler/Oceanborne** (diver@gem.co.za) and **Glen Curtis**, for **Struik Image Library/SIL,** with the exception of the individual photographers or agencies listed below.

Cover photograph: **Al Hornsby.**

Andy Belcher (www.legendphotography.co.nz): pp5, 6, 8, 9, 10, 23, 33, 41 (left), 49, 63, 75, 82 (bottom left), 83, 85 (bottom), 90, 91 (left and right).

Garmin: p68.

Jack Jackson: pp36 (left), 46 (top right), 69, 84 (top and bottom), 85 (top left and right), 87 (top and bottom), 89 (centre).

Anthony Johnson/SIL: front cover flap, pp37, 42, 43 (top), 47 (top), 39, 40, 41, 67, 64 (top).

Stefania Lamberti: p26.

Suunto: p72.

Peter Pinnock: p71.

Geoff Spiby: pp38, 88.

SIL: Struik Image Library, Cape Town (email: carmen@struik.co.za).